Henry Van Dyke

Straight Sermons to Young Men and Other Human Beings

Preached before the universities of Yale, Harvard and Princeton

Henry Van Dyke

Straight Sermons to Young Men and Other Human Beings
Preached before the universities of Yale, Harvard and Princeton

ISBN/EAN: 9783337114466

Printed in Europe, USA, Canada, Australia, Japan

Cover: Foto ©Lupo / pixelio.de

More available books at **www.hansebooks.com**

By Henry Van Dyke.

THE POETRY OF TENNYSON. *Third Edition.* $2.00.

STRAIGHT SERMONS: To Young Men and other Human Beings. $1.25.

THE REALITY OF RELIGION. *Fifth Edition*, $1.00.

THE STORY OF THE PSALMS. *Fourth Edition.* $1.50.

STRAIGHT SERMONS

STRAIGHT SERMONS

To Young Men and Other Human Beings

PREACHED BEFORE THE UNIVERSITIES OF
YALE HARVARD AND PRINCETON

BY

HENRY VAN DYKE D. D.
PASTOR OF THE BRICK CHURCH
NEW YORK

NEW YORK
Charles Scribner's Sons
1893

Copyright, 1893,
By HENRY VAN DYKE.

All rights reserved.

The Riverside Press, Cambridge, Mass., U. S. A.
Electrotyped and Printed by H. O. Houghton & Company.

TO THE MEMORY OF

PHILLIPS BROOKS

A NOBLE MAN AMONG MEN

A FAITHFUL PREACHER OF CHRIST

AND A TRUE SHEPHERD OF SOULS

THIS BOOK IS DEDICATED

PREFACE

"And the crooked shall be made straight."

Isaiah xl. 4.

IT has not seemed necessary, and perhaps it would not be possible, to disguise the contents of this small volume as essays, or to set it forth under a general and taking title which might offer some allurement to curiosity. Let it go for what it is, — a book of sermons, straight and simple.

They were made for a church in which, fortunately, there are a great many young men, and they have since been preached, with one exception, in college chapels at Harvard, Yale, Princeton, and elsewhere. This fact is mentioned merely to account for their practical tendency, and to explain, or excuse, the singular circumstance that there is nothing peculiar in their religious teaching.

This singularity arises from the conviction, which I cherish, that young men are really human beings. They are not a distinct species. They belong to the human race and are entitled to be humanly treated. The best life for them is not separate and artificial, but natural, simple, active, full of vigorous exercise for mind and body. The right education for them is not that of the cloister, in which they are divided from the world, but that of the home, the school, the university, the camp, the workshop, the athletic field, the market-place, where liberty is joined to responsibility, and where they are taught to feel that they belong to the world and trained to play a noble, manly part in it. The true religion to guide them in this education, and fit them for this life, is not something novel and peculiar, specially devised for young men, but simply the plain religion of Christ, which is good for everybody, of every age and condition, and for all alike.

It is good for all of us human beings to know that we are not creatures of chance or fate, but children of God, capable of fellowship with Him, and heirs of immortality if we will only hold fast to our birthright. It is good for us all to have firm faith and true courage; to pray for power from above; and to live as those who have been redeemed by Christ from the bondage of sin and selfishness and moral death. It is good for us all to take warning and encouragement from the mistakes and adventures of other men, and to bring the life-histories of the Bible home to our own business and bosoms. It is good for us all to refrain from harsh and hasty judgment of our fellow-men, and to imitate what Francis of Assisi calls "the great Courtesy of God, who maketh his sun to shine and his rain to fall upon the just and upon the unjust." It is good for us all not to waste our time in speculating about those mysteries of theology which lie beyond the horizon, but rather to content ourselves with proving the value of a short creed, honestly believed and thoroughly applied. This, in outline, is the kind of religion which my father (of blessed memory) taught to me, and which I have tried to teach in these sermons.

But there is one thing in which they have been distinctly influenced by the character of the congregations to whom they were preached. No thinking minister can stand up before a company largely composed of young men without a strong wish to be plain-spoken and to come straight to the point. They have a fine impatience of all mere formalities and roundabout modes of speech, which acts as a moral tonic to brace the mind from vagueness and cleanse the tongue of cant. They want a man to say what he means and to mean what he says. The influence of this unspoken demand is wholesome and inspiring, and the preacher ought to show his gratitude for it by honestly endeavouring to meet it.

For this reason I have tried to write these sermons, not in a theological dialect, but in the English language.

Their real aim is nothing else than to help people to be good, which is the hardest and the finest thing in the world. Their gospel is simply this: that the sure way to be good is to trust and follow Jesus Christ, the Son of God.

MINISTER'S ROOM, HARVARD COLLEGE,
January, 1893.

CONTENTS.

		PAGE
I.	A Man	1
II.	Faith	27
III.	Courage	51
IV.	Power	71
V.	Redemption	97
VI.	Abraham's Adventure	123
VII.	Solomon's Choice	147
VIII.	Peter's Mistake	167
IX.	God over All	191
X.	The Horizon	211

I

A MAN

"How much, then, is a man better than a sheep?"
Matthew xii. 12.

"How much, then, is a man better than a sheep?"

To Him who first spoke these noble words they were an exclamation; for He knew, as no one else has ever known, "what was in man." But to us, who repeat them, they often seem like a question; for we are so ignorant of what is best in ourselves and our fellow-men, we have so confused ourselves with artificial views and theories, that we find ourselves at the point to ask in perplexity, How much, then, is a man better than a sheep?

It is evident that the answer to this question must depend upon the view that we take of life. And at the very outset I want to invite your attention to two of the views that are current in the world, and the necessary conclusions to which they lead us in regard to man.

Suppose, in the first place, that we take a

materialistic view of life. We shall then deny all evidence except that which we receive through our senses. Looking at the world from this standpoint, we shall see in it a great mass of matter, curiously regulated by laws which have results but no purposes, and agitated into various modes of motion by a secret force whose origin is, and forever must be, unknown. Life, in man as in other animals, is but one form of this force. Rising through many subtle gradations from the first tremor that passes through the gastric nerve of a jelly-fish to the most delicate vibration of gray matter in the brain of a Plato or a Shakespeare, it is really the same from the beginning to the end, — physical in its birth among the kindred forces of heat and electricity, physical in its decay and extinction as the causes which sustain it are gradually weakened or suddenly cut off. The only difference between man and the other animals is a difference of degree. The ape takes his place in our ancestral tree, and with the sheep we must acknowledge at least a cousinship.

It is true that we have somewhat the advantage of these poor relations. We belong to the more fortunate branch of the family, and have entered upon an inheritance considerably enlarged by the extinction of collateral branches. But, after all, it is the same inheritance; and there is nothing in humanity which is not derived from, and destined to, earth and ashes and dust.

If, then, you accept this view of life, what answer can you give to the question, How much is a man better than a sheep? You must say: He is a little better, but not much. In some things he has the advantage. He lives longer, and has more powers of action and capacities of pleasure. He is more clever, and has succeeded in making the sheep subject to his domination. But the balance is not all on one side. The sheep has fewer pains, as well as fewer pleasures; less toil, as well as less power. If it does not know how to make a coat, at least it succeeds in growing its own natural wool clothing, and that without taxation. Above all, the sheep is not troubled with any of those vain dreams of moral responsibility and future life which are the cause of such great and needless trouble to humanity. The flocks that fed in the pastures of Bethlehem got just as much physical happiness out of existence as the shepherd David who watched them; and, being natural agnostics, they were free from David's errors in regard to religion. They could give all their attention to eating, drinking, and sleeping, which is the chief end of life. From the materialistic standpoint, a man may be a little better than a sheep, but not much.

Or suppose, in the second place, that we take the commercial view of life. We shall then say that all things must be measured by their money value, and that it is neither profitable nor necessary to inquire into their real nature or their essential worth. Men and sheep are worth what they will bring in the open market; and this depends upon the supply and demand. Sheep of a very rare breed have been sold for as much as five or six thousand dollars. But men of common stock, in places where men are plenty and cheap (as for example in Central Africa), may be purchased for the price of a rusty musket or a piece of cotton cloth. According to this principle, we must admit that the comparative value of a man and a sheep is a very uncertain matter, and that there are times when the dumb animal is much the more valuable of the two.

Of course, you perceive that this view, carried out to its logical conclusions, means slavery; and you call my attention to the fact that slavery has been abolished, by common consent of the civilized world. Yes, thank God, that is true. We have done away with the logical conclusion. In this land, at least, men and sheep are no longer put up at the same block to be disposed of to the highest bidder. We have gotten rid of the logical conclusion. But have we gotten rid entirely of the premise on which it rested? Does not the commercial view of life still prevail in civilized society?

"How much is that man worth?" asks the curious inquirer. "That man," answers the animated Commercial Registry and Business Directory, "is worth a million dollars; and the man sitting next to him is not worth a penny." What other answer can be given by one who judges everything by a money standard? If wealth is really the measure of value, if the end of life is the production or the acquisition of riches, then humanity must take its place in the sliding scale of commodities. Its value is not fixed and certain. It depends upon accidents of trade. We must learn to look upon ourselves and our fellow-men purely from a business point of view, and to ask only : What can this man make ? how much has that man made ? how much can I get out of this man's labour ? how much will that man pay for my services ? Those little children that play in the squalid city streets, — they are nothing to me or to the world ; there are too many of them, they are worthless. Those long-fleeced, high-bred sheep that feed upon my pastures, they are among my most costly possessions, they will bring an enormous price, they are immensely valuable. How much is a man better than a sheep ? What a foolish question! Sometimes the man is better; sometimes the sheep is better. It all depends upon the supply and demand.

Now these two views of life, the materialistic and the commercial, always have existed and do still exist in the world. Men have held them consciously and unconsciously. At this very day there are some who profess them; and there are many who act upon them, although they may not be willing to acknowledge them. They have been the parents of countless errors in philosophy and sociology; they have bred innumerable and loathsome vices and shames and cruelties and oppressions in the human race. It was to shatter and destroy these deadly falsehoods, to sweep them away from the mind and heart of humanity, that Jesus Christ came into the world. We cannot receive his gospel in any sense, we cannot begin to understand its meaning and purpose, unless we fully, freely, and sincerely accept his great revelation of the divine dignity and inestimable value of man as man.

We say this was his revelation. Undoubtedly it is true that Christ came to reveal God to man. But undoubtedly it is just as true that He came to reveal man to himself. He called himself the Son of God, but He called himself also the Son of Man. His nature was truly divine, but his nature was no less truly human. He became man. And what is the meaning of that lowly birth in the most helpless form of infancy, if it be not to teach us that humanity is so related to Deity that it is capable of receiving and embodying God himself? He died for man.

And what is the meaning of that sacrifice, if it be not to teach us that God counts no price too great to pay for the redemption of the human soul? This gospel of our Lord and Saviour Jesus Christ contains the highest, grandest, most ennobling doctrine of humanity that ever has been proclaimed on earth. It is the only certain cure for low and debasing views of life. It is the only doctrine from which we can learn to think of ourselves and our fellow-men as we ought to think. And I ask you to consider for a little while to-day the teachings of Jesus Christ in regard to the dignity and worth of a man.

Suppose, then, that we come to Him with this question: How much is a man better than a sheep? He will tell us that a man is infinitely better, because he is the child of God, because he is capable of fellowship with God, and because he is made for an immortal life. And this threefold answer will shine out for us not only in the words, but also in the deeds, and above all in the death, of the Son of God and the Son of Man.

I. Think, first of all, of the dignity of a man, as the offspring and the likeness of

God. This was not a new doctrine first proclaimed by Christ. It is clearly taught in the magnificent imagery of the Book of Genesis. The chief design of that great picture of the beginnings is to show that a Personal Creator is the source and author of all things that are made. But next to that, and almost, perhaps altogether, of equal importance, is the design to show that man is incalculably superior to all the other works of God, — that the distance between him and the lower animals is not a difference in degree, but a difference in kind; yes, the difference is so great that we must use a new word to describe the origin of humanity, and if we speak of the stars and the earth, the trees and the flowers, the fishes, the birds and the beasts, as the works of God, when man appears we must find a nobler name and say, This is more than God's work, it is God's child.

Our human consciousness confirms this testimony and answers to it. We know that there is something in us which raises us infinitely above the things that we see and hear and touch, and the creatures that appear at least to spend their brief life in the automatic workings of sense and instinct. These powers of reason and affection and conscience, and above all this wonderful power of free will, the faculty of swift, sovereign, voluntary choice, belong to a higher being. We say not to corruption, Thou art my father, nor to the worm, Thou art my mother; but to God, Thou art my father, and to the Great Spirit, In thee was my life born. Frail and mortal as our physical existence may be, in some respects the most frail, the most defenseless among animals, we are yet conscious of something that lifts us up and makes us supreme. "Man," says Pascal, "is but a reed, the feeblest thing in nature; but he is a reed that thinks. It needs not that the universe arm itself to crush him. An exhalation, a drop of water, suffice to destroy him. But were the universe to crush him, man is yet nobler than the universe, for he knows that he dies, and the universe, even in prevailing against him, knows not its power."

Now the beauty and strength of Christ's doctrine of man lie not in the fact that He was at pains to explain and defend and justify this view of human nature, but in the fact that He assumed it with an unshaken conviction of its truth, and acted upon it always and everywhere. He spoke to man, not as the product of Nature, but as the child of God. He took it for granted that we are different from plants and animals, and that we are conscious of the difference. "Consider the lilies," He says to us, "the lilies cannot consider themselves: they know not what they are, nor what their life means; but you know, and you can draw the lesson of their lower beauty into your higher life. Regard the birds of the air: they are dumb and unconscious dependents upon the Divine bounty, but you are conscious objects of the Divine care; are you not of more value than many sparrows?" Through all his words we feel the thrilling power of this high doctrine of humanity. He is always appealing to reason, to conscience, to the power of choice between good and evil, to the noble and God-like faculties in man.

And now think for a moment of the fact that his life was voluntarily, and of set purpose, spent among the poorest and humblest of mankind. Remember that He spoke not to philosophers and scholars, but to peasants and fishermen and the little children of the world. What did He mean by that? Surely it was to teach us that this doctrine of the dignity of human nature applies to man as man. It is not based upon considerations of wealth or learning or culture or eloquence. Those are the things of which the world takes account, and without which it refuses to pay any attention to us. A mere man, in the eyes of the world, is a nobody. But Christ comes to humanity in its poverty, in its ignorance, stripped of all outward attributes and signs of power, destitute of all save that which belongs in common to mankind, — to this lowly child, this very beggar-maid of human nature, comes the King, and speaks to her as a princess in disguise, and sets a crown upon her head. And I ask you if this simple fact ought not to teach us how much a man is better than a sheep.

II. But Christ reveals to us another and a still higher ground of the dignity of man by speaking to us as beings who are capable of holding communion with God, and reflecting the divine holiness in our hearts and lives. And here also his doctrine gains clearness and force when we bring it into close connection with his conduct. I suppose that there are few of us who would not be ready to admit at once that there are some men and women who have high spiritual capacities. For them, we say, religion is a possible thing. They can attain to the knowledge of God and fellowship with Him. They can pray, and sing praises, and do holy work. It is easy for them to be good. They are born good. They are saints by nature. But for the great mass of the human race, this is out of the question, absurd, impossible. They must dwell in ignorance, in wickedness, in impiety.

But to all this Christ says, No! No, to our theory of perfection for the few. No, to our theory of hopeless degradation for the many. He takes his way straight to the outcasts of the world, the publicans and the harlots and sinners; and to them He speaks of the mercy and the love of God and the beauty of the heavenly life: not to cast them into black despair; not because it was impossible for them to be good and to find God, but because it was divinely possible, — because God was waiting for them, and because something in them was waiting for God. They were lost, — but surely they never could have been lost unless they had first of all belonged to God; and this makes it possible for them to be found again. They were prodigals, — but surely the prodigal is also a child, and there is a place for him in the father's house. He may dwell among the swine, but he is not one of them; he is capable of remembering his father's love, he is capable of answering his father's embrace, he is capable of dwelling in his father's house in filial love and obedience.

That is the doctrine of Christ in regard to fallen and disordered and guilty human nature. It is fallen, it is disordered, it is guilty; but the capacity of reconciliation, of holiness, of love to God, still dwells in it, and may be quickened into a new life. That is God's work, but God himself could not do it if man were not capable of it.

Do you remember the story of the portrait of Dante which is painted upon the walls of the Bargello, at Florence? For many years it was supposed that the picture had utterly perished. Men had heard of it, but no one living had ever seen it. But presently came an artist who was determined to find it again. He went into the place where tradition said that it had been painted. The room was used as a storehouse for lumber and straw. The walls were covered with dirty whitewash. He had the heaps of rubbish carried away. Patiently and carefully he removed the whitewash from the wall. Lines and colours long hidden began to appear. And at last the grave, lofty, noble face of the great poet looked out again upon the world of light.

"That was wonderful," you say, "that was beautiful!" Not half so wonderful as the work which Christ came to do in the heart of man, — to restore the likeness of God and bring the divine image to the light. He comes to us with the knowledge that God's image is there, though concealed; He touches us with the faith that the likeness can be restored. To have upon our hearts the impress of the divine nature, to know that there is no human being in whom that treasure is not hidden, and from whose stained and dusty soul Christ cannot bring out that reflection of God's face, — that, indeed, is to feel the dignity and value of humanity, and to know that a man is better than a sheep!

III. There is yet one more element in Christ's teaching in regard to the dignity and value of man; and that is his doctrine of immortality. This truth springs inevitably out of his teaching in regard to the origin and capacity of human nature. A being formed in the divine image, a being capable of reflecting the divine holiness, is a being so lofty that he must have also the capacity of entering into a life which is not dependent upon the nourishment of meat and drink, and in which the spiritual powers shall be delivered from the bondage of sense and the fear of death, so that they may be unfolded to perfection. All that Christ teaches about man, all that Christ offers to do for man, links him to a vast and boundless future.

This idea of immortality runs through everything that Jesus says and does. Never for a moment does He speak to man as a creature of this present world. Never for a moment does He forget, or suffer us to forget, that our largest and most precious interests lie in the world to come. He would arouse our souls to perceive and contemplate the immense issues of life. The perils that beset us here through sin are not brief and momentary dangers, possibilities of disgrace in the eyes of men, of suffering such limited pain as our bodies can endure in the disintegrating process of disease, of dying a temporal death, which at the worst can only cause us a few hours of anguish. A man might bear these things, and take the risk of this world's shame and sickness and death, for the sake of some darling sin. But the truth that flashes on us like lightning from the word of Christ, is that the consequence of sin is the peril of losing an immortal spirit. " I will forewarn you," says He, " whom ye shall fear: fear Him which after he hath killed hath power to cast into hell; yea, I say unto you, fear Him."

On the other hand, the opportunities that come to us here, through the grace of God, are not merely opportunities of temporal peace and happiness, they are chances of securing endless and immeasurable felicity, wealth that can never be counted or lost, peace that the world can neither give nor take away. We must understand that now the kingdom of God has come near unto us. It is a time when the doors of heaven are open. We may gain an inheritance incorruptible and undefiled, and that fadeth not away. We may lay hold, not only on a present joy of holiness, but on an everlasting life with God.

It is thus that Christ looks upon the children of men, not as herds of dumb driven cattle, but as living souls moving onward to eternity. It is thus that He dies for men, not to deliver them from brief sorrows, but to save them from final loss, and to bring them into bliss that knows no end. It is thus that He speaks to us, in solemn words before which our dreams of earthly pleasure and power and fame and wealth are dissipated like unsubstantial vapours: "What shall it profit a man if he gain the whole world and lose his own soul? or what shall a man give in exchange for his soul?"

There never was a time in which Christ's doctrine of the dignity and value of a man as man was more needed than it is to-day. There is no truth more important and necessary for us to take into our hearts, and hold fast, and carry out in our lives. For here we stand in an age when the very throng and pressure and superfluity of human life lead us to set a low estimate upon its value. The air we breathe is heavy with materialism and commercialism. The lowest and most debasing views of human nature are freely proclaimed and unconsciously accepted. There is no escape, no safety for us, save in coming back to Christ, and learning from Him that man is the child of God, made in the divine image, capable of the divine fellowship, and destined to an immortal life. I want to tell you just three of the practical reasons why we must learn this.

We need to learn it in order to understand the real meaning, and guilt, and danger, and hatefulness of sin.

Men are telling us, nowadays, that there is no such thing as sin. It is a dream, a delusion. It must be left out of account. All the evils in the world are natural and inevitable. They are simply the secretions of human nature. There is no more shame or guilt connected with them than with the malaria of the swamp, or the poison of the nightshade.

But Christ tells us that sin is real, and that it is the enemy, the curse, the destroyer of mankind. It is not a part of man as God made him; it is a part of man as he has unmade and degraded himself. It is the marring of the divine image, the ruin of the glorious temple, the self-mutilation and suicide of the immortal soul. It is sin that casts man down into the mire. It is sin that drags him from the fellowship of God into the company of beasts. It is sin that leads him into the far country of famine, and leaves him among the swine, and makes him fain to fill his belly with the husks that the swine do eat. Therefore we must hate sin, and fear it, and abhor it, always and everywhere. When we look into our own hearts and find sin there, we must humble ourselves before God, and repent in sackcloth and ashes. Every sin that nestles within us is a part of the world's shame and misery. Every selfish desire that stirs within our souls is a part of that which has stirred up strife, and cruelty, and murder, and horrible torture, and bloody war among the children of men. Every lustful thought that defiles our imagination is a part of that which has begotten loathsome vices and crawling shames throughout the world. My brother-men, God hates sin because it ruins man. And when we know what that means, when we feel that same poison of evil within us, we must hate sin as He does, and bow in penitence before Him, crying, "God be merciful to me a sinner."

We need to learn Christ's doctrine of the dignity and value of humanity in order to help us to love our fellow-men.

This is a thing that is easy to profess, but hard, bitterly hard, to do. The faults and follies of human nature are so apparent, the unlovely and contemptible and offensive qualities of many people thrust themselves so sharply upon our notice and repel us so constantly, that we are tempted to shrink back wounded and disappointed, and to relapse into a life that is governed by its disgusts. If we dwell in the atmosphere of a Christless world, if we read only those newspapers which chronicle the crimes and meannesses of men, or those realistic novels which deal with the secret vices and corruptions of humanity, and fill our souls with the unspoken conviction that virtue is an old-fashioned dream, and that there is no man good, no woman pure, I do not see how we can help despising and hating mankind. Who shall deliver us from this spirit of bitterness?

Who shall take us by the hand and lead us out of this heavy, fetid air of the lazar-house and the morgue? None but Christ. If we will go with Him, He will teach us not to hate our fellow-men for what they are, but to love them for what they may become. He will teach us to look not for the evil which is manifest, but for the good which is hidden. He will teach us not to despair, but to hope, even for the most degraded of mankind. And so, perchance, as we keep company with Him, we shall learn the secret of that divine charity which fills the heart with peace, and joy, and quiet strength. We shall learn to do good unto all men as we have opportunity, not for the sake of gratitude or reward, but because they are the children of our Father, and the brethren of our Saviour. We shall learn the meaning of that blessed death on Calvary, and be willing to give ourselves as a sacrifice for others, knowing that he that turneth a sinner from the error of his ways shall save a soul from death and cover a multitude of sins.

Finally, we need to accept and believe Christ's doctrine of the dignity and value of humanity in order that it may lead us personally to God and a higher life.

You are infinitely better and more precious than the dumb beasts. You know it, you feel it, you are conscious that you belong to another world. And yet it may be that there are some of you who forget it, and live as if there were no God, no soul, no future life. Your ambitions are fixed upon the wealth that corrodes, the fame that fades; your desires are towards the pleasures that pall upon the senses; you are bartering immortal treasure for the things which perish in the using. The time is coming when you must lie down like the dumb beast and crumble into dust. Nay, not like the beast, for to you shall come in that hour the still, small voice saying, "This night shall thy soul be required of thee."

Thy soul, — why not think of it now? The image of God is impressed upon it. The one thing needful for you is to know, and love, and serve Him who is the father of your spirit.

Come then to Christ, who alone can save you from the sin which defiles and destroys your manhood. Come then to Christ, who alone can make you good men and true, living in the power of an endless life. Come then to Christ, that you may have fellowship on earth with the Son of Man, and dwell with the Son of God forever, and behold his glory.

FAITH

"*Without faith it is impossible to please Him.*"
Hebrews xi. 6.

"Without faith it is impossible to please Him."

THIS is a short statement of a large truth. The plain language lends force and dignity to the thought. It needs no embroidered words, no jewelry of speech, to set it off. For truth, like beauty, shows best with least adornment.

In trying to unfold the meaning of this text I would fain keep to that simplicity and clearness of which it gives us such a good model. There is no reason why religion should be made dark and difficult by talking about it in long, unfamiliar, antiquated words which cause people to wish for a dictionary; nor is there any excuse for seeking to win the wonder and astonishment of men by obscure sayings and curious comparisons, — mountains of eloquence which labour long and violently to produce a little mouse of practical sense. In ancient times the teachers of the people were told to read in the book of the Law of God distinctly, and give the sense, and cause the people to understand the meaning. To reach that result no pains are too great, no effort is too costly. I would rather spend five days in trying to make a text clear and level to the mind, to open the door of it so that any one could walk in, than five minutes in trying to make it strange and mysterious, to cover it with all kinds of ornaments and arabesques so that nobody should be able to find the keyhole and unlock the door.

Religion is full of mysteries. The object of the Bible is not to increase them, but to remove them. If a certain amount of mystery still remains, it lies in the subject, and not in the way in which it is treated. For the most part, the teachings and rules of the Scriptures are so clear and direct that the wayfaring man, though a fool, need not err therein; they shed light and not darkness; they disperse the clouds to reveal the sun.

Take the declaration of the text: "Without faith it is impossible to please God." How easy it is to see just why the writer of the Epistle to the Hebrews inserted that sentence where it stands! He is writing about the heroes of faith, — the men and women who, from the very beginning of the world, have been bound together into one company by this great principle of all true and noble life. Among them he counts the patriarch Enoch. But as we look back to the brief record of Enoch's life in the Book of Genesis we find that not a word is said there about his faith. By what right, then, is he included in the list? Why is he counted among the faithful? "I will tell you why," says the writer of the Epistle: "it is because he obtained this testimony, that he pleased God. This is proof positive that he must have had faith. Where you find a flower, you know there must have been a seed. Where you find a river, you know there must be a spring. Where you see a flame, you know there must be a fire. Where you find a man beloved and blessed of God, you know there must be faith. Whether it is recorded or not, whether you can see it or not, it must be there, germ of his virtue, fountain-head of his goodness, living source of warmth and light; for without faith it is impossible to please God."

How simple and how beautiful is that phrase, — to please God. What a sense of nearness to the Divine Being it gives us. How it discloses God's nature and character. What a noble statement of the true aim of life.

God can be pleased, then. He is not a cold abstraction, an immovable substance, a dull, unimpassioned, silent, joyless, mighty force. He is a person, capable of affections and emotions. He is a heart that feels. Delight is no stranger to Him. His love is no vague, blind impulse, flowing dumbly towards all things alike. It is a seeking, choosing love; and when it finds the object of its search, a thrill of gladness passes through it, larger, purer than we can understand, and yet like that which comes to us when we see the fairest and the best. He approves and blesses. His Spirit is filled with the music of pleasure.

To waken that music, to win that approval, to please God, — surely that is the highest and holiest object for a human life.

To please men is a natural impulse. There is no one who does not desire in some degree to obtain the liking and favour of his fellow-creatures. But presently, as we come to know by experience how shallow and how fickle are the fashions of the world, how false and often how impure are the motives by which the liking of the crowd is influenced, how easily it is gained by accident and lost by chance, we begin to see that this kind of surface favour is deceitful, and to look for something better.

To please good men, — that is a nobler ambition. To win the confidence and honour of those who are honest and earnest and upright; to speak some word, to do some deed, to exercise some virtue, of which those who think deep thoughts, and lead pure lives, and perform noble actions, shall say, " That was right, that was true, that was kind, that was brave," — this is a motive which has always been potent in the most generous breasts, restraining them from evil, nerving them to heroic efforts, stimulating them to dare and to do.

But there is a motive deeper and more intense than even this: it is the desire to please that one among our fellow-creatures whom we have chosen, it may be, as the most loyal heart and true; to pluck some flower from the lofty crags of duty; to win some honourable trophy in the world's great battlefield,—yes, even though that trophy be but the scar received in warring for the right, the banner which has been torn and stained in an unequal conflict, but never dishonoured; to do something, to endure something, which shall really please the one who is to us the best and dearest on earth,— how many a soul has been quickened, and uplifted, and strengthened to face danger, disgrace, and death by that profound desire!

But to please God, the perfect, radiant Being, the most wise, the most holy, the most beautiful, the most loving of all Spirits; to perform some task, achieve some victory, bring some offering that shall be acceptable to Him, and in which He shall delight; simply to live our life, whatever it may be, so that He, the good and glorious God, shall approve and bless it, and say of it, " Well done," and welcome it into the sense of His own joy,— that is a divine ambition.

> " What vaster dream could hit the mood
> Of love on earth?"

It has sustained martyrs at the stake, and comforted prisoners in the dungeon, and cheered warriors in the heat of perilous conflict, and inspired labourers in every noble cause, and made thousands of obscure and nameless heroes in every hidden place of earth. It is the pillar of light which shines before the journeying host. It is the secret watchword of the army, given not to the leaders alone, but flashing like fire through all the ranks. When that thought descends upon us, it kindles our hearts and makes them live. What though we miss the applause of men; what though friends misunderstand, and foes defame, and the great world pass us by? There is One that seeth in secret, and followeth the soul in its toils and struggles, —the great King, whose approval is honour, whose love is happiness; to please Him is success, and victory, and peace.

There are a million ways of pleasing Him, as many as the characters of men, as many as the hues and shades of virtue, as many as the conflicts between good and evil, as many as the calls to honest labour, as many as the opportunities of doing right and being good. That is the broad meaning of this eleventh chapter of the Hebrews, with its long roll of different achievements, with its list of men and women of every age, of every quality and condition, slaves and freemen, leaders and followers, warriors and statesmen, saints and sinners, and silent martyrs, and nameless conquerors; there are a million ways of pleasing God, but not one without faith. Numberless forms of energy, but none without heat. Myriad colors of beauty, but none without light. All is cold and black until the sun shines. A universe of possibilities of goodness spreads before you, but not one of them can be realized unless you have faith. For without faith it is impossible to please God.

But why should this be so? Is it an arbitrary requirement which the Divine Being makes of his creatures, or is there a deep reason for it in the nature of men and the conditions of human life? I do not believe that God is ever arbitrary. He is indeed omnipotent, and He has the power to demand of us whatsoever He will. But there is always a wise and holy reason in his demands. Sometimes we cannot understand it; it lies too deep for us. But sometimes we can understand it; it lies within our reach. And in the present case I think we can easily see just why faith is necessary to the success of every effort to please Him.

Faith is not a strange and far-away thing which can only be explained to us by a revelation. It is a principle of common life. We exercise it every day. It is simply the confidence in something which is invisible; as the Apostle says, "it is the substance of things hoped for, the evidence of things not seen." Every time you receive the testimony of your fellow-men, every time you trust in the qualities of their character which are beyond the reach of your vision, every time you rely upon a law of logic in an argument, upon a law of nature in your action, upon a law of morality in your conduct, you exercise faith. It is the condition of reason, of activity, of human society. "All polities and societies," says a wise observer, "have come into existence through the trust of men in each other," and, we may add, through their trust in unseen principles of equity, and in future results of prudence, and in One higher than themselves whom they could neither see nor name. Take away confidence in the invisible, and the whole fabric decays, crumbles, and falls in ruin.

Thus, even from the human point of view, faith is necessary. But from the Divine point of view, it must appear infinitely more essential.

Man is made to know as much as possible, to do as much as possible, and to be as good as possible. In the sphere of knowledge, in the sphere of action, in the sphere of character, faith is the one element that gives life and power to please God.

I. Look first at the sphere of knowledge, the understanding of the world and of life. We stand in a strange and mysterious universe, with certain faculties to help us to a comprehension of it. First, we have the senses, and they tell us how things look, and taste, and sound, and feel. Then we have the reasoning powers, and they enable us to discover how things are related to each other, how causes are followed by effects, how great laws control their action and reaction. But is there not something beyond this, a depth below the deep and a height beyond the height? Every instinct of our nature assures us that there must be. The lesson of modern thought is the limitation of science and philosophy. But outside of this narrow circle lie the truths that we most desire and need to know. In that unexplored world dwells God. Why should we hesitate to confess that we must have another and a higher faculty of knowledge? The astronomer has keen eyes, but he knows their limitation, and he does no discredit to them when he uses the telescope to bring near the unseen stars. The entomologist has quick sight, but he does not disparage it when he turns to the microscope to search a drop of water for its strange, numberless forms of life. Reason is excellent and forceful, but beyond its boundaries there is a realm which can only be discerned by faith. Where science ends, where philosophy pauses, faith begins.

"By faith we understand that the worlds have been framed by the word of God, so that what is seen hath not been made out of things which do appear."

Mark the words: By faith we understand. It is a principle of comprehension, then, not of confusion; something which clarifies and enlarges the vision. It discloses not only the origin but also the purpose and the meaning of things. It is not the contradiction, but the crown and complement of reason. How can God be pleased with any knowledge from which this element is left out?

Suppose that you had written a book, and some one should take it up and measure it, and say: "This curious object is composed of cloth, paper, ink, glue, and thread. It is seven inches long, five inches wide, and two inches thick; it contains five hundred pages and a hundred thousand words, and I wonder where it came from and what it is for." Would that please you?

Suppose that you had carved a statue, and some one should find it and say: "This remarkable stone is composed of carbonate of lime; it is very smooth and white, and it weighs about six hundred pounds, and I think I have explained it perfectly." Would that satisfy you? Would you not be better pleased with the child, or the ignorant peasant, who stood and looked at your statue and felt its beauty, and recognized that it had been made by some one to represent a great, a noble, a lovely idea?

The world was made for its meaning, to show forth the wisdom, power, and goodness of God. If we do not see that, we see nothing.

We may be able to tell how many stars are in the Milky Way; we may be able to count the petals of every flower, and number the bones of every bird; but unless faith leads us to a deeper understanding, a more reverent comprehension of the significance of the universe, God can no more be pleased with our knowledge than the painter is pleased with the fly which touches his picture with its feelers, and sips the varnish from the surface, and dies without dreaming of the meaning, thought, feeling, embodied in the colours. But on the simplest soul that feels the wonder and the hidden glory of the universe, on the child to whom the stars are little windows into heaven, or the poet to whom

> "the meanest flower that blows can give
> Thoughts that do often lie too deep for tears,"

God looks down with pleasure and approval. For in such a soul He sees the beginning of faith, which is able to pass behind the appearance to the reality, and make its possessor wise unto everlasting life.

II. Turn now to the sphere of action. Here faith is no less necessary. There are some who would persuade us that believing is appropriate only to infancy and old age; that it is a kind of dreaming, an infirmity of the weak and visionary. But the truth is otherwise. Carlyle says: "Belief is great, life-giving. The history of a nation becomes fruitful, soul-elevating, great, so soon as it believes. A man lives by believing something, not by debating and arguing about many things." Faith is power. It makes men strong, ardent, persistent, heroic. Nothing truly great has ever been done in any department of the world's work without faith. Think of the faith of our explorers and discoverers,— Columbus, who found the New World; the Pilgrim Fathers, who planted it with life; Livingstone, who opened a new continent to civilization. Think of the faith of our men of science, — Galileo, Kepler, Newton, Faraday, Henry. Think of the faith of the reformers,— Wyclif, Luther, Knox. Think of the faith of the martyrs, — Polycarp, Huss, Savonarola, the Covenanters of Scotland, the Huguenots of France. Faith is a force, and those who grasp it lay hold of something which is able to make them mightier than themselves.

Let a man fasten himself to some great

idea, some large truth, some noble cause, even in the affairs of this world, and it will send him forward with energy, with steadfastness, with confidence. This is what Emerson meant when he said, " Hitch your wagon to a star." These are the potent, the commanding, the enduring, the inspiring men, — in our own history, men like Washington and Lincoln. They may fall, they may be defeated, they may perish; but onward moves the cause, and their souls go marching on with it, for they are part of it, they have believed in it.

And if the cause be divine, if the idea come from above, if the action be impelled by faith in God and a resolve to do his will, then how dauntless and impregnable does it make the heart in which it dwells! Paul standing alone against the mocking, sneering world to testify to the truth as it is in Jesus, " I believe and therefore speak: " Luther riding into the city of Worms, though every housetop were thronged with devils, and appearing alone before the imperial council, " Here stand I, I cannot do otherwise, God help me: " Morrison, the first missionary to China, standing alone on the deck of the ship that bears him to a strange and hostile world: "Do you think," says the captain, "that you will make an impression upon 400,000,000 Chinese?" "No, sir," is the reply, "but I believe that God will:" — that is faith, — everywhere and always the victory that overcometh the world.

I will make a personal confession to you. Very often it seems to me as if there were one, and only one, great and essential difference among the multitudes of people who inhabit this earth. Moving about among them, coming into contact with them, I find that some men and women seem unreal, hollow, visionary, masks without faces, costumes without character. They run in the grooves of custom, they drift to and fro on the currents of fashion, they are blown up and down by the winds of popular opinion; even when they seem to lead, it is only as the lightest leaf is carried along foremost by the gale. They are only animated shadows, without principle or probity, without conviction or consistency, without faith or fidelity. But other men and women seem real, and true, and genuine. There is something behind their looks, their words, their actions. They have power to touch, and move, and satisfy the heart, because they believe. Have you never felt the difference? Do you think that God does not feel it? Can a mask, a shadow, however fair or orderly, please Him? Will He withhold his approval and blessing from any real, honest, struggling, believing soul?

But perhaps some may be thinking just now: "This is the old story that the preacher is telling us; he is singing the same old song about faith, — and still faith, — and always the necessity of faith! Why not lay more emphasis on works? Surely they are more important. He has just told us that there are many ways of pleasing God. There are many courses of good conduct open to us all. If we follow any one of them, that is enough. So long as a man's actions are right it makes no difference what lies behind them, it makes no difference whether he believes or not." Do you really think so? Is there no difference between a body without a spirit and a body with a spirit? Does not the thought, the motive, the purpose count for something?

Here are a multitude of people giving their

money to support the Temple. And many rich men, standing beside the treasury, cast in their gifts; from habit, from a desire to appear well before the world, from a hope of reward. A poor widow comes with her two mites; she knows her gift will be despised, she fears it may be laughed at, but she believes that God wants her to do what she can, and that He will not refuse her offering. So her coppers fall in among the gold and the silver, and the Lord of the treasury blesses her, and says, "She hath given more than they all."

Here are two women going down to work among the sick and the poor. One goes because there is a fashion of it, because she would fain have the credit which belongs to the lady bountiful. She moves among them like an iceberg, and they hate her. She brings a chill with her which all her coals and blankets can never warm away. The other goes because she believes in it, believes that God wants her to do it, believes that the sorrowful and the distressed are Christ's brethren, and that she is bound to them, and that they have immortal souls which she may win for Him. She moves among them like a sister of Jesus and a friend of God; and of her the Master says, " Inasmuch as she hath done it unto one of the least of these my brethren, she hath done it unto me."

Here are two men praying. One stands upon the corner of the street, correct, punctilious; at the appointed time he lifts his hands, he raises his voice that he may be heard of men. The other kneels in the dust, ignorant, stammering, feeble; he lifts his face to Christ and says, " Lord, I believe, help thou mine unbelief." And that broken, stammering cry of honest faith pleases God, and brings the blessing which would never come to the Pharisee though he stood on the street corner till the crack of doom.

Let us never be so foolish as to think that it makes no difference whether we believe or not. Faith is the soul of conduct; faith is the bloom, the breath, the vital power of religion; without it, virtue is the alabaster box, empty; faith is the precious ointment whose fragrance fills the house. Therefore without faith it is impossible to please God.

III. Finally, faith is necessary because it is the only possible way of contact between God and man, the only way in which He can draw near to us, and save and bless us. And that, if you will believe it, is the one thing that He most desires to do. There is no compulsion laid upon Him. He does not act as one who is performing an indifferent task. He is so good that He longs to deliver us from sin and death, to bring us to himself, to give us a place in his happy kingdom. This is his glory and his delight: to rescue the perishing, to raise the fallen, to forgive the sinful, to give life to the dying. He loves this work so much that He sent his own dear Son into the world to accomplish it. And nothing that you can do will please Him so much as simply to let Him save you, and help you to be good.

Think for a moment: what can you do for any one who does not trust you, who does not believe in you? Nothing. That barrier of mistrust stands like a wall of ice between you and the soul that you desire to help. Is there anything that wounds you more than to be doubted and denied, and thrust away in suspicion or indifference? Truly that is the deepest and most bitter pain. Is there anything that pleases you more than to be trusted, — to have even a little child look up into your face, and put out its hand to meet yours, and come to you confidingly? By so much as God is better than you are, by so much more does He love to be trusted.

Yes, I know you are trying to be good, — fitfully, imperfectly, yet still trying. But there is something else that God would have you do first. He would have you believe that He wants you to be good, that He is willing to help you to be good, that He has sent his Son to make you good.

There is a hand stretched out to you, — a hand with a wound in the palm of it. Reach out the hand of your faith to clasp it, and cling to it, for without faith it is impossible to please God.

III

COURAGE

"Wait on the Lord: be of good courage, and he shall strengthen thine heart."

Psalm xxvii. 14.

"Wait on the Lord: be of good courage, and he shall strengthen thine heart."

This is a sermon about courage, one of the simplest and most straightforward of the virtues; necessary, and therefore possible, for every true and noble human life.

It is a quality that we admire by instinct. We need no teacher to tell us that it is a fine thing to be brave. The lack of courage is universally recognized as a grave defect in character. If in our own hearts we feel the want of it, if we cannot find enough of it to enable us to face the dangers and meet the responsibilities and fight the battles of life, we are not only sorry, but secretly ashamed. The absence of courage is a fault that few are willing to confess. We naturally conceal it, and cover it up, and try to keep it secret even from ourselves. We invent favourable names for it, which are only unconscious excuses. We call it prudence, or respectability, or conservatism, or economy, or worldly wisdom, or the instinct of self-preservation. For in truth there is nothing that we are more reluctant to admit than cowardice; and there is no virtue which we would more gladly possess and prove than courage.

In the first place, it is an honourable virtue. Men have always loved and praised it. It lends a glory and a splendour to the life in which it dwells, — lifts it up and ennobles it, and crowns it with light. The world delights in heroism, even in its rudest forms and lowest manifestations. Among the animals we create a sort of aristocracy on the basis of courage, and recognize, in the fearlessness of the game beasts and birds and fishes, a claim to rank above the timorous, furtive, spiritless members of creation.

And in man bravery is always fine. We salute it in our enemies. A daring foe is respected, and though we must fight against him we can still honour his courage, and almost forget the conflict in our admiration for his noble bearing. That is what Dr. Johnson meant by saying, "I love a good hater." The enemy who slinks and plots and conceals — makes traps and ambuscades, seeks to lead his opponent into dangers which he himself would never dare to face — is despicable, serpentine, and contemptible. But he who stands up boldly against his antagonist in any conflict, physical, social, or spiritual, and deals fair blows, and uses honest arguments, and faces the issues of warfare, is a man to love even across the chasm of strife. An outspoken infidel is far nobler than a disguised skeptic. A brave, frank, manly foe is infinitely better than a false, weak, timorous friend.

The literature of courage has always been immensely popular, and the history of the brave is written in letters of gold. It is this that men have loved to read in the strange, confused annals of war, — deeds of self-forgetful daring which leap from the smoke and clamour of battle, and shine in the sudden making of splendid names. It is the quality which levels youth with age, gives to woman the force of manhood, equalizes the peasant with the noble, and consumes all outward distinctions in the flame of glory. The boy Casabianca keeping the solitary deck of the burning vessel rather than disobey his father's commands; the brave Lady Douglas thrusting her tender arm through the staple of the door to defend her king from the assassin; Leonidas at Thermopylæ, and Horatius at the bridge, and the Six Hundred at Balaklava; old Cranmer bathing his hands in fire at the martyr's stake, and young Stephen praying fearlessly for his murderers; Florence Nightingale facing fever in Crimean hospitals; Father Damien braving leprosy in the Islands of the Sea; young men and maidens, old men and matrons, fighting, suffering, achieving, resisting, enduring, daring, living, and dying — it is the spark of heroism that kindles their names into the blaze of light, for everywhere and always courage is an honourable virtue.

In the second place, courage is a serviceable virtue. There is hardly any place in which it is not useful. There is no type of character, no sphere of action, in which there is not room and need for it.

Genius is talent set on fire by courage. Fidelity is simply daring to be true in small things as well as great. As many as are the conflicts and perils and hardships of life, so many are the uses and the forms of courage. It is necessary, indeed, as the protector and defender of all the other virtues. Courage is the standing army of the soul which keeps it from conquest, pillage, and slavery.

Unless we are brave we can hardly be truthful, or generous, or just, or pure, or kind, or loyal. " Few persons," says a wise observer, "have the courage to appear as good as they really are." You must be brave in order to fulfil your own possibilities of virtue. Courage is essential to guard the best qualities of the soul, and to clear the way for their action, and make them move with freedom and vigour.

" Courage, the highest gift, that scorns to bend
To mean devices for a sordid end ;
Courage, an independent spark from Heaven's throne,
By which the soul stands raised, triumphant, high, alone ;
The spring of all true acts is seated here,
As falsehoods draw their sordid birth from fear."

If we desire to be good, we must first of all desire to be brave, that against all opposition, scorn, and danger we may move straight onward to do the right.

In the third place, courage is a comfortable virtue. It fills the soul with inward peace and strength ; in fact this is just what it is, — courage is simply strength of heart. Subjection to fear is weakness, bondage, feverish unrest. To be afraid is to have no soul that we can call our own; it is to be at the beck and call of alien powers, to be chained and driven and tormented; it is to lose the life itself in the anxious care to keep it. Many people are so afraid to die that they have never begun to live. But courage emancipates us and gives us to ourselves, that we may give ourselves freely and without fear to God. How sweet and clear and steady is the life into which this virtue enters day by day, not merely in those great flashes of excitement which come in the moments of crisis, but in the presence of the hourly perils, the continual conflicts. Not to tremble at the shadows which surround us, not to shrink from the foes who threaten us, not to hesitate and falter and stand despairing still among the perplexities and trials of our life, but to move steadily onward without fear, if only we can keep ourselves without reproach, — surely that is what the Psalmist meant by good courage and strength of heart, and it is a most comfortable, pleasant, peaceful, and happy virtue.

Let us talk together for a while about this virtue and consider what we mean by it, how we can obtain it, and what good it will do us.

I. First of all, let us try to understand the difference between courage and some of the things which are often mistaken for it.

There is a sharp distinction between courage and recklessness. The reckless man is ignorant; he rushes into danger without hesitation, simply because he does not know what danger means. The brave man is intelligent; he faces danger because he understands it and is prepared to meet it. The drunkard who runs, in the delirium of intoxication, into a burning house is not brave; he is only stupid. But the clear-eyed hero who makes his way, with every sense alert and every nerve strung, into the hell of flames to rescue some little child, proves his courage.

The more keenly we are awake to the perils of life, the higher and grander is the possibility of being truly brave. To drift along, as some people do, through this world of sin, as if there were nothing in it to fear; to slide easily downward, as some people do, to the gate of death, as if there were nothing beyond it to fear; to sport and dance, and eat and drink and sleep, as some people do, under the arch of heaven, as if there were no One above it to fear, — what is this but the part of the fool who hath said in his heart, "There is no God, there is no sin, there is no judgment"? But to face the temptations and perplexities and dangers of the world without yielding to fear; to pass, without trembling, by the dark portals of the grave in a faith that is stronger than fear; to dare to live in the presence of the holy, mighty God in the confidence of a love that casteth out fear, — that is courage.

Then there is another sharp distinction between courage and insensibility. Some natures are so constituted that they do not feel pain very keenly. Their nerves are sluggish and deeply hidden. This may be an advantage or a disadvantage; for certainly, if they escape some possibilities of suffering, they must also lose many possibilities of enjoyment. But one thing is sure: to persons of this temperament, fear is comparatively a stranger. They can move forward almost with indifference in situations where a more sensitive nature would be profoundly agitated. Now we must not suppose for a moment that this insensibility makes them brave. It simply exempts them in some measure from the necessity of courage. The bravest soul is that which feels the tremor and resists it, shrinks from the flame and faces it. Never was a better soldier than the old French marshal Montluc, who said that he had often gone into battle shaking with fear, and had recovered courage only when he had said a prayer. A pale face, a trembling hand, yes, even a heart that stands still with dread, may belong to a hero who is brave enough to carry them into the midst of conflict without faltering or failing, straight on to victory or death. Courage does not consist in the absence of fear, but in the conquest of it.

Take it in little things. Here is the great, dull, heavy dray-horse; what is it for him to move stolidly on through noises which do not alarm him, and past strange objects which he does not notice? But when the high-mettled, keen-sensed thoroughbred goes through the same tumult, and past the same objects, with every nerve and muscle quivering, that is courage. It demands no great effort for the *voyageur*, who is inured to hardships and trained to steadiness, to guide his frail canoe through the foaming rapids. But for a woman who is by nature sensitive and timid, to sit quiet and silent in the boat, not because she has no fear, but because she will not yield to it, — that is brave.

The same thing is true in moral trials. There are some people to whom reproach and ridicule and condemnation mean little. They simply do not care; they are pachydermatous. But there are others to whom the unkind word is like a blow, and the sneer like a sword-thrust, and the breath of contempt like the heat of flames; and when they endure these things and face them, and will not be driven by them from the path of duty, they are truly courageous.

Do you understand what I mean? Timidity is no more inconsistent with courage than doubt is inconsistent with faith. For as faith is simply the overriding and subjugating of doubt by believing where you cannot prove, so courage is simply the conquest and suppression of fear by going straight on in the path of duty and love.

There is one more distinction that needs to be drawn, — the distinction between courage and daring. This distinction is not in kind, but in degree. For daring is only a rare and exceptional kind of courage. It is for great occasions; the battle, the shipwreck, the conflagration. It is an inspiration; Emerson calls it "a flash of moral genius." But courage in the broader sense is an every-day virtue. It includes the possibility of daring, if it be called for; but from hour to hour, in the long, steady run of life, courage manifests itself in quieter, humbler forms, — in patience under little trials, in perseverance in distasteful labours, in endurance of suffering, in resistance of continual and familiar temptations, in hope and cheerfulness and activity and fidelity and truthfulness and kindness, and such sweet, homely virtues as may find a place in the narrowest and most uneventful life.

There is no duty so small, no trial so slight, that it does not afford room for courage. It has a meaning and value for every phase of existence; for the workshop and for the battlefield, for the thronged city and for the lonely desert, for the sick-room and for the market-place, for the study and for the counting-house, for the church and for the drawing-room. There is courage physical, and social, and moral, and intellectual, — a soldier's courage, a doctor's courage, a lawyer's courage, a preacher's courage, a nurse's courage, a merchant's courage, a man's courage, a woman's courage, — for courage is just strength of heart, and the strong heart makes itself felt everywhere, and lifts up the whole of life, and ennobles it, and makes it move directly to its chosen aim.

II. Now, if this is what we mean by courage, how are we to obtain it? What is it that really strengthens the heart and makes it brave?

Well, there are many lesser things that will help us, such as a simple and wholesome physical life, plain food and vigorous exercise, a steady regard for great moral principles and ideas, a healthful course of reading, a sincere friendship with brave and true and single-minded men and women, a habit of self-forgetfulness and consecration to duty. But of these things I have not time to speak, for there is something greater and better than any of these, — something which in fact includes them all and sums them up in a a word, "Wait on the Lord." That is the truest and deepest source of courage. To believe that He is, and that He has made us for himself; to love Him, and give ourselves up to Him, because He is holy and true and wise and good and brave beyond all human thought; to lean upon Him and trust Him and rest in Him, with confidence that He will never leave us nor forsake us ; to work for Him, and suffer for his sake, and be faithful to his service, — that is the way to learn courage.

Without God what can you do ? You are a frail, weak, tempted, mortal creature. The burdens of life will crush you, the evils of sin will destroy you, the tempests of trouble will overwhelm you, the darkness of death will engulf you. But if you are joined to God, you can resist and endure and fight and conquer, in his strength. This is what the Psalmist means in the text, "Wait on the Lord, be of good courage, and He shall strengthen thy heart." So runs our translation. The scholars tell us that it ought to read, " Be of good courage and let thy heart be strong." But the meaning is the same. For the courage comes from the waiting on God, and He is the giver of strength to the heart.

"If it had not been the Lord who was on our side, now may Israel say, then the proud waters had gone over our souls." It was the Lord who stood by them and sustained them through the storm. Hear Paul: "If God be for us, who can be against us?" And again, "I can do all things through Christ who strengtheneth me." And then hear Christ: "My meat is to do the will of Him that sent me, and to finish his work." That is the secret of courage. The lamp that is joined to the electric current glows with light. The soul that is joined to the infinite source of courage in God, burns steadfast, serene, and inextinguishable through life and death.

III. And now let us ask, how will that divine courage help us if we obtain it? What will it do for us?

Everything. There is no good thing that we really desire and need that will not be brought nearer to us by this strength of heart. Every day and every hour of our lives it will be a help, a joy, a treasure, a blessing to us.

You men have to go through with your daily toil, and face the perplexities of business life, and resist the temptations to dishonesty and meanness and uncleanness which touch you on every side. You must be brave, and if you are brave in Christ you will win.

You women have to meet your daily household cares, and suffer the pains and trials which belong to a woman's life, and restrain your lips from scandal and your hearts from jealousy and envy, and keep your souls up above the deadening influences of luxury and frivolity and fashion. You must be brave, — never does courage shine more brightly than in a true woman, — and if you are brave you will " adorn the doctrine of God our Saviour " with the charm of pure, unselfish, lovely character and conduct which is a rebuke to all grossness of demeanour, and an encouragement to all knighthood and true chivalry. For such women men would even dare to die.

You boys and girls at school, young men and maidens at college, have to do your work honestly, and speak the truth fearlessly, and avoid evil companionship steadfastly, and live up to your principles modestly and firmly. You must be brave, and sometimes very brave, to do this, and if you have the right courage in the conflicts of youth you will be trained by them to play a noble part in the great battle of life.

And the preacher who speaks to you has to face the constant, exhausting demands of a minister's life, to declare the divine message without fear or favour, to search the Scriptures and tell men plainly what they teach, without regard to human traditions; caring nothing for old doctrines or new doctrines, but simply and solely for the truth as it is in Jesus, and following it with absolute loyalty whithersoever it may lead. Surely the man who has to do this needs courage, in order that he may be neither ashamed of the old nor afraid of the new, but always faithful to the true.

Indeed, we all have the same need. For every one of us, there is nothing more desirable, nothing more necessary, than real strength of heart. If we can obtain it from the divine and only source, it will make our lives straight and clean and fine. It will enable us to follow Jesus of Nazareth, who was not only the purest and the gentlest, but also the bravest Spirit that ever dwelt on earth.

And do you think, if that kind of courage comes into our hearts, — the courage of faith, which believes in spite of difficulties, and fights its way through doubt to a firmer assurance; the courage of confession, which overcomes all dread of ridicule or reproach, and is not ashamed of Christ nor of his words, but ready to preach the Gospel at Rome also; the courage of life, which goes on trying to be good in spite of failures, and holding fast to the ideal in spite of temptations, and warring for the right in spite of heavy odds, and bearing the appointed burden in spite of weariness, straight through to the end: do you think the courage of death will fail us? We do not know when we shall have to meet that last conflict, that ultimate adventure. But when the hour comes, if we have been brave enough to live aright, we shall be brave enough to die at peace.

"Sunset and evening star,
 And one clear call for me!
And may there be no moaning of the bar,
 When I put out to sea,

"But such a tide as moving seems asleep,
    Too full for sound and foam,
When that which drew from out the boundless deep
    Turns again home!

"Twilight and evening bell,
    And after that the dark!
And may there be no sadness of farewell,
    When I embark!

"For tho' from out our bourne of Time and Place
    The flood may bear me far,
I hope to see my Pilot face to face
    When I have crost the bar."

IV

POWER

"O God, thou art my God; early will I seek thee: my soul thirsteth for thee. . . . To see thy power and thy glory, so as I have seen thee in the sanctuary."

Psalm lxiii. 2.

"That I may know Him, and the power of his resurrection."

Phil. iii. 10.

"To see thy power and thy glory, so as I have seen thee in the sanctuary."

"That I may know Him, and the power of his resurrection."

Here are two men separated by centuries, — the psalmist of the old dispensation and the apostle of the new dispensation, — uttering the deepest desire of their hearts. In both of them we find that there is an earnest and ardent longing to see, to know, the power of God. In both of them there is the recognition of a place, a way, in which that power is manifested and in which it may be discerned; in both of them there is the confident expectation that the knowledge of that power, when it is attained, will be potent in its spiritual effect upon their lives.

Now we may be quite sure that the thing for which David and Paul longed so ardently is something which we also ought to desire, and pray for, and seek after. If they needed it, we need it. If it was possible for them to find it, it is possible for us. If it was good for them, it will be good for us. Let us think about it for a little while; for it is only by thinking about great and good things that we come to love them, and it is only by loving them that we come to long for them, and it is only by longing for them that we are impelled to seek after them, and it is only by seeking after them that they become ours and we enter into vital experience of their beauty and blessedness.

Is not this the reason why our lives often seem so narrow and poor and weak, why they have such a sense of limitation and constriction in them, why their interests seem so trivial, their possibilities so small, their results so feeble, why we often appear to ourselves barren in thought and dry in feeling, empty of hope and bankrupt in power? Is it not because we think so much of the things that are petty and narrow and barren and transient, and so little of the things that are great and fruitful and glorious and eternal? These dry and thirsty lives of ours, these dull, stale, flat, and unprofitable lives of ours, these paltry lives, — whose fault is it that they are so? Ours, and ours alone. For the riches of an infinite wealth and the powers of an immeasurable strength are all about us waiting for us to possess and use them. But there is only one way in which we can enter into their possession, and that is by thinking about them, by considering them earnestly and steadily until they draw us to themselves.

The strength of your life is measured by the strength of your will. But the strength of your will is just the strength of the wish that lies behind it. And the strength of your wish depends upon the sincerity and earnestness and tenacity with which you fix your attention upon the things which are really great and worthy to be loved. This is what the Apostle means when he says, at the close of his description of a life which is strong, and inwardly renewed, and growing in glory even in the midst of affliction, — "while we look not at the things which are seen, but at the things which are unseen." It is while we look that we learn to love. It is by loving that we learn to seek. And it is in seeking that we find and are blessed.

Let us be sure, then, that it is no mere profitless speculation about mysteries of no practical value to which our double text invites us. It is a thought that enriches, ennobles, strengthens, blesses. It is a meditation by which our lives will be enlarged and uplifted and invigorated. It is for the sake of a joy which will be like music in our souls among life's discords; it is for the sake of a strength of spirit which will be to us like a wind from heaven sending us forward on our course as ships that cleave the waves and triumph against the tides; it is in order that we may "have life, and have it more abundantly," that we are asked to think about the powerful knowledge of the power of God.

I. We may inquire, first, why should we wish to see and know the power of God?

Well, it seems to me that the vision of power is always wonderful and admirable and, in a certain sense, beautiful, and therefore a thing to be desired for its own sake. The perception of a mighty force in action, even in the physical world, confers a high and noble pleasure on the mind. When the force is sudden and violent, as in the case of a great tempest, our pleasure in beholding it is mixed with awe, it is a solemn and trembling delight; it may be overshadowed with fear, or with pity for the misfortunes of those who have been overwhelmed by the storm; yet the force in itself is magnificent, and the sight of it thrills and expands the soul. But when it is an orderly and beneficent force that we behold, then the vision is one of pure and unmingled joy. How glorious, for example, is the sight of a great river sweeping down from its source among the mountains to its resting-place in the sea. How it forces its way among the hills, cutting through the rocks and carving a channel for itself in the solid earth, leaping boldly from the cliffs, and rushing down the steep inclines with an energy which needs but to be harnessed to do the work of a million men, — this is power, we say, power visible, and it is a grand thing to see. And the same thing is true of the resistless tides of the ocean on which we look with unending wonder and pleasure; true also of the might of the imprisoned giant Steam as we see it whirling the wheels of some great engine and driving the vast ship by day and night through leagues of rolling waters.

But it is far more true of those forces which are more silent and secret, like the heat of the sun, or the force of gravitation. We become aware of these forces not so much through our senses alone as through our thought, our inward perception. Look at a blade of corn cleaving the ground, and remember that all over the world countless millions upon millions of them are pushing upward with a power which taken altogether is simply incalculable; and all this lifting of tons of bread out of the earth to the hand of man is simply the drawing of the sun that shines above you. Look at the starry heavens on a clear still night; companies, regiments, battalions, armies of worlds, all marching without haste and without rest, keeping pace in their majestic orbits; and the force that binds them to their courses is the same that quietly loosens the ripened apple from the bough and drops it at your feet. Surely a thought like this is a vision of power, and it is good for the soul.

But it is doubly good to know that it is all the power of God. To understand that all the mighty energy which throbs and pulses through the universe, comes from Him, that force is but the effluence of his will, and law but the expression of his wisdom; to stand before some vast manifestation of power in nature and feel that it is only an infinitesimal fraction, only a passing play of the omnipotence of God; to see Him hurl Niagara into the gulf more easily than you would pour a glass of water on the ground, — is good for the soul. It humbles and exalts. It begets that awe of spirit which is essential to true religion. We want a mighty God, one who can hold the winds and the waves in the hollow of his hand. And for our own sake, for the sake of a deeper reverence and a firmer confidence towards Him, we ought to wish to see the evidence of divine power in the great elemental forces of nature.

But there is another kind of power still more wonderful, still more impressive than that of which we have been speaking. It is spiritual power, — the power which is manifested in the conquest of evil, in the triumph of virtue, in the achievements and victories of a moral being. This is grander and more admirable than any physical force that has ever acted upon the universe of matter.

"For tho' the giant ages heave the hill
 And break the shore, and evermore
Make and break, and work their will;
Tho' world on world in myriad myriads roll
 Around us, each with different powers
 And other forms of life than ours,
What know we greater than the soul?"

The vision of spiritual power, even as we see it in the imperfect manifestations of human life, is ennobling and uplifting. The rush of courage along the perilous path of duty is finer than the foaming leap of the torrent from the crag. Integrity resisting temptation overtops the mountains in grandeur. Love, giving and blessing without stint, has a beauty and a potency of which the sunlight is but a faint and feeble image. When we see these things they thrill us with joy; they enlarge and enrich our souls.

And if that is true, how much more satisfying and strengthening must it be to behold the spiritual power of God? For God also is a soul, the Great Soul; the essence of his being is not physical but moral; and the secret of his strength is in his holiness, righteousness, justice, goodness, mercy, and love. To know something of the force of the great Spirit; to see that there is no temptation that can even shake the strong foundation of his equity, no evil that can finally resist the victorious sweep of his holy will, no falsehood that can withstand the penetrating flash of his truth, nothing that can limit or exhaust the great tide of his love; to catch sight of the workings of One who is omnipotent against all foes and therefore triumphant over the last enemy, death, — that is a vision of joy and power far beyond all others, and therefore it is to be desired and prayed for and sought after with the whole heart.

But, after all, we have not yet touched the deepest and strongest reason why we should long to see and know the power of God. We have been moving hitherto upon the surface; let us pierce now to the centre. The great reason why we need to consider God's power is because we are utterly dependent on that power for the salvation of our souls. Without it there is no peace, no hope, no certainty. Unless God is mighty to save, we can never be saved.

The religion of the Bible differs from all others in two points. The first is, that it makes salvation the hardest thing in the world. The second is, that it makes salvation the easiest thing in the world.

How lofty, how inaccessible is the standard of holiness revealed in this religion. How immense are its requirements and conditions. Other religions set before us ideals which seem by comparison like the foothills of the Jura, somewhat more elevated indeed than the surrounding valleys, but still smooth and easy, with gradual paths and footholds. But Christianity lifts Mont Blanc before our eyes, serene, remote, awful in its dazzling splendour, and bids us climb to holiness without which no man shall see God. "Be ye perfect, even as your father which is in heaven is perfect." What hope is there of attaining to that shining height?

I wonder if any of you have ever had the feeling that has come to me in reading Christ's Sermon on the Mount. It is a feeling of great distance and almost intolerable remoteness, — a feeling as if one should come to a mighty cliff, towering far up into heaven, crowned with eternal beauty and radiance, and hear a voice crying from that far height, "Come up hither and dwell with me!" When I listen to those wonderful beatitudes, when I hear those searching demands for a purity which is stainless in deed, in word, in thought, and in feeling, when I see how strait is the gate and how narrow is the way that leadeth unto life, a sense of utter helplessness sweeps through me and my spirit is overwhelmed within me.

And is not the same thing true even when we take shorter and more limited views of the duties and requirements of the Christian life? Here are these faults and vices and evil habits with which we have been struggling. We have used all the force that we have against them, and yet they are not extirpated. How shall they ever be conquered? Is it not a hopeless conflict? Here we have been trying to do our duty, and putting all our hearts into the effort to be good and to do good, and yet so little is accomplished, so far do we come short. More must be done; we must be better; we must live higher and holier and more useful lives. But where is strength to come from since we have already used all that we possess? How shall we overcome greater difficulties when we have already taxed ourselves to the uttermost in coming thus far? how render larger service when we have already strained our powers to the breaking-point? Next year's temptations, how shall we conquer them? Next year's work, how shall we do it?

Not even the wise and needful reminder that the Christian life is gradual is sufficient to deliver us from this sense of helplessness. It is true, of course, that "heaven is not reached at a single bound," that only to-day's burdens are to be borne to-day, that growth in grace is like the blade and the ear and the full corn in the ear; and it helps us immensely to remember this. But, after all, this does not quite reach the heart of our trouble. Even a power which is to be gradually exercised has its limits. Steam can do so much, and no more. Electricity can do so much, and no more. But the Christian life is unlimited; it rises forever; it advances without end; its goal is perfection. What does it profit the blade of corn to go on maturing its poor little kernels, if at last it will be required to bear some celestial and imperishable fruit? What does it advantage the pilgrim to climb painfully the lower slopes, if the summit of the pass is inaccessible? Some little human goodness, some advance in virtue, we may perhaps attain; but a perfect holiness is out of our reach. Look at heaven, — a kingdom of unsullied love; look at the life of the glorified saints, sorrowless, tearless, sinless, dwelling in perfect and deathless fellowship with God, — is not that beyond our power?

Yes, it is; and yet it is the ideal set before us in the word of God; and therefore we say that the Bible makes salvation the hardest thing in the world, makes it something that would be impossible and hopeless, if it did not at the same time make it easy and accessible and possible for every human soul. For this is what the Bible does: it reveals that our salvation is all of God; it reveals that the power that worketh in us is his power, and that it is able to do exceeding abundantly above all that we can ask or think.

And now we can see the real reason why the Psalmist and the Apostle prayed so earnestly to know the power of God, and why the truest and best of human souls have always repeated that prayer in many forms and in many languages, and why we ought to take it up and make it truly our own.

It is because that power is our hope and our salvation. David was a strong man, but he knew that he could never conquer sin in his own strength. Paul was a strong man, but he knew that he was often unable to do the things that he would; he knew that he was not sufficient for these things; the spirit was willing, but the flesh was weak; he felt that he was bound like a captive to a body of sin and death. And so they both longed and cried, so we should long and cry, to know something greater than human strength, even the power of the mighty God unto salvation.

II. Well, then, we come to our second question: How may this spiritual power of God be known?

There is a twofold answer; and yet it is really one, for both parts of it belong together, and the latter supplements and completes the former, even as the sunrise is the fulfilment of the dawn.

The Psalmist says, "My soul thirsteth for thee, to see thy power and thy glory, even as I have seen thee in the sanctuary." By this I think he means that the power of God may be known in the experiences of religion. Not only in his own soul, as he has confessed his sin and found pardon, as he has prayed for help and been strengthened, as he has asked for deliverance and been lifted out of the horrible pit and the miry clay, as he has implored guidance and been led in a plain path, — not only in his own soul, but also in the souls of his brother-men who have been delivered in the same perils, and helped in the same conflicts, and strengthened in the same sanctuary by humble faith and earnest prayer and true surrender to the Spirit of God, the Psalmist has seen the workings of Divine power, and so he longs to see them again.

The same vision is open to us. Every grace that God has given to us in the past, every touch of his life that has quickened us, every assistance of his Spirit that has supported us and given us a victory over evil, is a proof and evidence of his power. Let us remember and trust.

Was it long ago, or was it but yesterday, that we came to Him with that heavy weight of sin, and, asking for relief, found it? Come then, and, kneeling at his feet to-day, with a yet heavier load, it may be, prove the same almighty strength to deliver from sin. Was it long ago, or was it yesterday, that we felt that thrill of new life, of consecration, of devotion passing through us as we gave ourselves to God? Come then, and, renewing the gift to-day, feel again the same touch of power. Was it long ago, or was it but yesterday, that we prayed for strength to perform a certain duty, to bear a certain burden, to overcome a certain temptation, and received it? Do we dream that the Divine force was exhausted in answering that one prayer? No more than the great river is exhausted by turning the wheels of one mill. Put it to the proof again with to-day's duty, to-day's burden, to-day's temptation. Thrust yourself further and deeper into the stream of God's power, and feel it again, as you have felt it before, able to do exceeding abundantly. Remember and trust. "Thou hast been my help: leave me not, neither forsake me, O God of my salvation."

But there are times when these memories of power experienced in the past grow faint and dim, times when it seems that all we can see behind us is a long succession of failures, and all we can feel now is a pervading sense of weakness. At such times it is good to consider the mighty things which God has wrought in and through other lives. He has lifted the hands that hung down, and strengthened the feeble knees. He has made the evil good; the sinful, pure; the selfish, generous; the base, noble. He has made apostles and saints out of men and women that the world would have thrown away as rubbish. Why, the whole New Testament is just a record of that, — Peter, the weak and wayward; Mary Magdalen, the defiled; Zaccheus, the worldly; Thomas, the despondent; Paul, the persecutor and blasphemer. What God could do in the first century, He can do, He is doing, to-day.

What is it that we want? Is it faith to conquer doubt? There are men and women all around us believing in the face of difficulties greater than ours. Is it patience under trials? There are men and women all around us who are bearing trials as heavy as ours without a murmur. Is it usefulness? Consider the mighty works that God has wrought through the hands of man. Think of the great influence of the thousands of Sunday-schools scattered all over the world. How did that begin? In the efforts of poor printer Robert Raikes to teach the ragged children of Gloucester. Think of the beautiful charity which carries vast multitudes of little ones every summer out of the crowded city into the fresh air of the country. How did that begin? In the attempt of a country minister to bring a score of poor children to spend a few days in the farmhouses of his scanty parish. What can we do? Nothing. What can God do with us? Anything; whatsoever He will.

But perhaps you will say, "This does not help me so much, after all. For these men and women are separated from me. I do not really know them, nor they me. There is no bond between us, nothing to make me partaker of their life. In fact, they are so far above me that it humiliates me even to think of them, and if they knew me there is no reason to think that they could do anything else than look down upon me in my selfishness, weakness, and sin."

To one who is in this state of mind I think Paul is more helpful than David, the New Testament more precious than the Old. Let us turn, then, to the way in which the apostle sought to know and feel the power of God. "That I may know Him," he cried, that is Christ, "and the power of his resurrection." And in another place he said: "That ye may know what is the exceeding greatness of his power to us-ward who believe, according to the working of his mighty power which He wrought in Christ when He raised Him from the dead." That is the true proof and manifestation of the spiritual power of God; the life and resurrection of Jesus Christ, conqueror of sin and death.

Remember that it is a real human life, lived in the same flesh and blood, under the same conditions and limitations as ours, made human in order that it might be like ours. Remember that the strength of it is not physical but spiritual, the same Spirit of God dwelling in Jesus whom God promises to give to all that ask Him. Remember that its triumph over falsehood and temptation and sin and death is one triumph, and that the resurrection is but the final working of the same power which worked all through the holy life of Jesus, so that He conquered the grave with the same might with which He overcame evil. Remember that this life is given to us and for us, so that we may belong to it, as the branches belong to the vine, as the members belong to the body. Remember that Christ says: "Without me ye can do nothing, but lo! I am with you alway, even unto the end of the world. He that believeth on me, the works that I do shall he do also. Where I am, there shall ye be also." Remember these things, and we shall understand what Paul means by knowing the power of his resurrection. It is to know that the greatest spiritual power in the universe, the power which made Jesus Christ perfect in holiness, is ready to enter and work in us, and that He who raised up Jesus from the dead shall quicken our mortal bodies by his Spirit that dwelleth in us.

III. Now what practical effect will this knowledge of the mighty power of God have in our lives? David thinks chiefly of one effect; Paul chiefly of another.

The prominent thought in the psalm is the joy that comes from seeing God's power: "My soul shall be satisfied as with marrow and fatness, and my mouth shall praise thee with joyful lips." And surely that is a good thing. Joy is essential to true religion. A gloomy religion is far from God. A sad gospel is a contradiction in terms, like a black sun. "Behold," said the angel, "I bring you good tidings of great joy, which shall be to all people." And that message was simply the news of a great power which had appeared in the world for salvation. David, indeed, did not hear this message in its fulness, did not see this power in its perfection. But he heard the promise of it, he felt the thrill of its coming. His hope was in God. "I have set the Lord always before me; because He is at my right hand I shall not be moved. Therefore my heart is glad and my glory rejoiceth; my flesh also shall rest in hope." Yes, God is light, God is love, God is power; and therefore God is hope.

Little does he know of true joy who knows not this. Lightly, foolishly, falsely does he think of the great resistant force of evil, the tremendous difficulties of being good, the vast inertia of a world lying in sin, who exults in aught else than the knowledge of a Divine power able to overcome it all. When we look at the follies and vices and crimes and shames which still exist among men, when we see the immense obstacles which stand in the way of the spiritual progress of humanity, when we discern the dark and sullen and obstinate influences which are potent in our own hearts, despair for ourselves and for the world seems natural, pessimism right and inevitable. Will the slender ray of light that shines on the mountain-top ever conquer the huge darkness?

Well, that depends on the source from which it springs. If it comes only from a fire kindled there by human hands, it will go out again when the fuel is exhausted. But if it comes from the sun, it will grow until the night is vanquished. And that is what the Bible tells us. Behind every manifestation of spiritual life there is the Spirit. Behind Christianity there is Christ. Behind Christ there is God. For He is the brightness of the Father's glory, and the express image of his person; and the power that works in Him, the power that has raised Him from the dead and set Him at God's right hand in heavenly places, is the power that is saving every one that believeth, and reconciling the world to God. When we know that, despair ceases to exist, and joy fills the heart with music.

But in Paul's mind there is another thought. It is the thought of the strength, the vigour, the energy that come from this knowledge. "This one thing I do," he says: "forgetting those things which are behind, and reaching forth unto those things which are before, I press toward the mark for the prize of the high calling of God in Christ Jesus." And elsewhere, again and again, he expresses the same thought. At the close of that glorious chapter on the resurrection, in the First Epistle to the Corinthians, he says: "Therefore, my beloved brethren, be ye steadfast, immovable, always abounding in the work of the Lord." And again: "Work out your own salvation with fear and trembling, for it is God which worketh in you." And again: "I can do all things through Christ which strengtheneth me."

That is the secret of strength; to know the Divine power and to use it. The man who does not use it cannot really know it.

The Christian who says, "I know the power of God, and I am trusting in that to save me, and sustain me, and make me useful, and bring me to heaven," and yet makes no real effort to be good or to do good, is like a man sitting on the bank of a mighty river, and casting chips upon its sweeping tide, and saying, "This river is able to bear me to my journey's end." What you need to do is to push your boat out into the current, and feel its resistless force, and move onward with it. Then you will know the power that now you only know about.

Is there any reason why our lives should be feeble and stagnant and worthless? Is there any reason why we should not overcome temptation and endure trial, and work the works of God in the world, and come at last to the height of his abode in heaven? Only one, — that we do not know Him who is able to do exceeding abundantly above all that we ask or think, according to the power that worketh in us. Lay hold on Him by faith and all things are possible. Let us clasp the hand of Christ and climb; and as we climb He will lift us out of sin, out of selfishness, out of weakness, out of death, into holiness, into love, into strength, into life, and we shall know the power of his resurrection.

V

REDEMPTION

"For ye are bought with a price."

1 *Corinthians* vi. 20.

"For ye are bought with a price."

The Apostle Paul thinks so much of this plain saying that he repeats it in the next chapter, as if to make sure that we should not forget it, nor fail to appropriate it in our lives. And in this he is right. For it is indeed a word like a jewel, shining, precious, imperishable. If we rightly estimate its worth, if we take it into the treasury of our hearts, it will more enrich and ennoble us than the possession of royal gems.

And yet it may seem strange to you that so much should be made of this saying. For what is it, after all, this confident and positive assertion of the apostle, but the statement of a great debt which we owe and can never pay — a tremendous obligation resting upon every one of us from which we can never escape? What does it tell us save that we have all been bought in the open market, as slaves are bought, — for so the

Apostle's word signifies, — and that the price has been paid, and that henceforth we belong to a master? Is not this a strange thing to rejoice over, as if it were a precious boon?

Certainly, it is a strange thing, but nevertheless it is a true thing; for, in regard to human life at least, truth is almost always stranger than fiction. That which is obvious and self-evident is frequently false, and generally superficial. It is only by striking down into the hidden depths of our nature that we come to those paradoxes in which the essence of truth resides. "He that findeth his life shall lose it." That is a contradiction in terms, but it is a reality in experience. "He that is greatest among you shall be your servant." That is a falsehood to the sense, but it is a truth to the soul. "He only is wise who knows himself to be a fool." To a little learning, that seems absurd, but to a profound philosophy it is the voice of wisdom. And so this saying of Paul's, which looks at first like a burden, an impoverishment, a chain, is in fact an uplifting, an enrichment, an emancipation, for those who really understand it and translate it into life.

Think of this for a moment, and try to see what it means. There is a great truth here, if we can only get it into words.

What is liberty? It is the recognition of voluntary allegiance to the highest law. And what is the highest law? It is the law of gratitude and love. Who, then, is free? He who sees and feels the obligations which bind him to serve the highest and the best. The noblest, richest, fullest, purest life is that which has the deepest and strongest sense of indebtedness resting upon it always, and impelling it forward along the line of duty, which is also the line of joy. So, then, true liberty is the highest kind of bondage.

Do you understand what I mean? Do these words of mine let even a glimmer of the truth shine through them? Let us try to see it a little more clearly. There are three broad statements in regard to this life of ours that I want to submit to you. You shall pronounce your own judgment upon their truth.

I. The sense of belonging to something is essential to our happiness.

We are never without this sense, and therefore we do not realize its importance. But let us try for once to strip it away from us, and then perhaps we may feel what it means. You remember the story of " The Man without a Country." Endeavor now to construct in imagination the figure of a man without a world, without a fellow-man, without a God. I do not mean that you should try to think the world and humanity and God out of existence, so that you should stand alone in the universe. That, indeed, would be the only complete isolation, for as long as anything existed, your consciousness of it would make some kind of a bond between you and it. But stop short, for the present, of the horrible insanity of absolute loneliness in void space, and attempt only to cut yourself off from connection with all things that exist, so that you shall have no dependence and no obligation outside of yourself.

You are independent. You have no parentage; for if you had, that would create a tie between you and those to whom you owed your being. You are not even the product of natural forces; for if they had produced you, you would owe something to them. You have no place in the universe; for if you had, you would be bound to fill it.

You are not in the thoughts of God, if there be a God; for if He thought of you, you would be responsible for meeting his thought. You are a rank outsider. You are superfluous, forgotten, obsolete, — "a looker-on in Vienna." All this mighty sum of "things forever working" goes on without you, and there is nothing for you to do; for if you were needed anywhere, that need would create an obligation; and since you are not needed, you dare not touch a finger to the work without presumption and interference. All these linked lives and related intelligences cling together and play into each other, and every one has a share in another and belongs to all the rest. But the chain is complete without you; you are not in it. You have neither relation nor religion, for both of them consist in a bond and create a bondage. You are an independent atom, an outcast fragment of some extinct universe, dropped by chance into this world where all things belong together, — a foundling, a homeless thing. For you alone belong — Nowhere, and are the forsaken child of — Nothing!

Does not the mere contemplation of such

a condition as that throw us back forcibly, almost violently, upon the truth that the joy of our life is a dependent joy, and that we can only come into true and happy possession of ourselves when we realize that we belong to something greater than ourselves? As living beings we are part of a universe of life; as intelligent beings we are in connection with a great circle of conscious intelligences; as spiritual beings we have our place in a moral world controlled and governed by the supreme Spirit. In each of these spheres there is a law, a duty, an obligation, a responsibility, for us. And our felicity lies in the discovery and acknowledgment of those ties which fit us and bind us to take our place, to play our part, to do our work, to live our life, where we belong.

II. This leads us on at once to the second proposition about life. The true uplifting and emancipation of our life comes through the recognition of the higher ties and relationships which bind us.

I mean that the progress and elevation of the soul is a process of discovering, not that it is independent and masterless, but that the lower laws and conditions under which it lives are subordinate to the higher laws, and that its bondage in a certain sphere becomes transformed into liberty when it is lifted up into a higher sphere, where both he that serveth and he that is served are subject unto a supreme sovereignty which is above all. That is what I understand by the reign of law, — not the domination of one rule alone upon all that is, but the reign of law over law, the higher above the lower, and the highest of all supreme; so that those who rise to that last and topmost height, where God forever dwells and is what He commands, are sharers in his liberty and dominion: they become the sons of God, not because they have cast off and renounced their obligations, but because they have recognized them step by step, sphere by sphere, until at last they come with glad submission into unity and harmony with that which is sovereign and ultimate; and that, if the Bible is true, is nothing else than perfect Love.

See how we can trace the steps of this process in the common life of man! The child, coming into existence, not by its own choice and will, but out of life behind it, becomes aware first of its physical being. It takes its place among the creatures that breathe and eat and sleep, and adapts itself spontaneously to the laws of that existence. A physical life has begun which will be continually dependent upon obedience to those laws. But presently another life begins to dawn within the first life. The child becomes conscious of powers of observation, of comparison, of thought. It does not cease to belong to the animal kingdom; it becomes, however, an animal who thinks, and thus is subject to the higher laws of reason; and it is only by following that law that the child is really lifted upwards, and grows intelligent and free. And then comes the opening of another world to which it belongs, — the spiritual world, — a disclosure so secret and vital that we cannot describe the order or manner of it. But we know the three channels through which it comes, — the affections, the conscience, and the religious feeling. And we know the signs and marks of it. We can tell when the child begins to feel the ties of love and duty which bind it to humankind, the laws of right and wrong which are different and superior to all other laws, the sense of awe and dependence and responsibility which is the evidence of God unseen. We know also that the growth of that child into liberty and nobility will depend upon the recognition of these invisible things, and the allegiance to them. It will rise, it will become a free and beautiful soul, only as it lives in love and duty and worship.

Take another illustration, simpler and more striking. Here is a slave bound by artificial law to the service of a human master. How shall you make that man free? Suppose you slay the master, and strike the bonds from the limbs of the slave, and say to him, "Go! you are free, you have no master, you belong to nobody." What have you done for him? Is he really any more free than he was before? Is he not still a slave, though a masterless one? But suppose you teach him to believe that he is a human being, and that he has a service to render, even in his low estate, to the whole brotherhood of mankind, — a service just as real and true, and therefore just as noble, as that of the king upon his throne. Suppose you bring into his mind the great truth that he belongs to God just as fully and as completely as his master does, and that, even under the hard conditions of his life, it is his duty, his privilege, his glory, to serve God by honesty and fidelity and diligence and purity. Now, indeed, you have liberated his soul; and if the liberation of his body comes, as it ought to come, as it must come, it will find him already a free man, and fit for liberty, because he has caught sight of the true meaning of fraternity and equality.

It was thus that Christianity advanced upon the world, and thus that it dealt with the evil of human slavery. Entering the mighty Roman Empire at a time when it included perhaps 120,000,000 of people and 60,000,000 of them slaves, it proclaimed no insurrection, it created no anarchy. It taught the Fatherhood of God and the brotherhood of man, not merely as a doctrine, but as a law of life binding all who believed in it. It said in plain words, by the mouth of Paul and all his fellow-servants of Christianity: "Art thou called, being a slave? Care not for it; but if thou mayest be made free, use it rather. For he that is called in the Lord being a slave, is the Lord's freeman; likewise also he that is called being free is Christ's slave." And so the Gospel carries written upon its very face the great truth that the only real deliverance from a lower bondage lies in the recognition of a higher obligation. Men are made free by discerning their noblest allegiance.

III. But there is yet one more truth that we must take into account if we are to grasp the whole of the subject, and find ourselves in a position to understand the divine beauty and meaning of the text. Let me try to utter it briefly and clearly.

The inward joy and power of our life, in every sphere, come from the discovery that its highest obligation rests at last upon the law of gratitude. In every tie that binds us we are made free and glad to serve, when we recognize that we have been " bought with a price."

Do you see what I mean? Take this thought of recognizing the price that has been paid for us, and carry it out into the different fields of human life, and see how it sheds a glory and a splendour on every relationship, on every duty, on every sacrifice.

Here is the family circle. You belong to it. It has its obligations and responsibilities for you. You are subject to your parents.

They have a right to control you and to demand your obedience. So far, you are subject to a law, good and necessary, but in itself external and formal. Presently you come to feel, if you are worth anything at all, that this family life has cost something; you catch a glimpse of the pangs of anguish, the hours of watching and weariness, the countless and continual draughts on life and love, that a mother has borne for your sake. You think of the daily toils, the struggles with adverse fortune, the cares and self-denials through which a father has passed, that you might be protected and nurtured and educated. You begin to understand that not only expenditures of such things as strength and money, but far greater treasures of the heart, affections, anxieties, prayers, sacrifices, expenditures of the very best of life, have been made for you. And when that truth comes to you, you feel that you are bought with a price. Does it oppress and darken your life? Does it not rather ennoble and gladden you? It lifts you up into the true filial relation,—makes you long to be a nobler son, a better daughter, more worthy of the sacrifices which have been made for you. If they could ever be repaid, they would be a burden until you had discharged the debt. But just because it is so great that it transcends payment, it makes you a willing debtor forever, and binds you to a grateful and loving life.

Is not the same thing true of our relations to our country? You are born a citizen of the republic; and that does not mean very much, as a bare fact, except a duty of paying taxes, and a privilege, which you may not prize very highly, of voting with more or less regularity. But suppose it flashes upon you some day, as I believe it does flash upon most honest and manly boys who read the history of their country, that all the hardships and perils and conflicts of the forefathers — all the patient endurance of privations and the brave defiance of dangers, all the offerings of treasure and blood that have been made to found, liberate, defend, and preserve our country — are a price paid for you. Do you not see how that thought must kindle the flame of patriotism upon the altar of your heart? How it must awaken that strange, inward warmth of feeling which glows at the very mention of your country's name? How it will rise, if you are a true man, in the hour of need, into that devotion which cries, "It is sweet and beautiful to die for one's country"? Surely the very soul of patriotism is this wonderful sense that we have been bought with a price.

And the same thing is true of our relationship to humanity, to the great brotherhood of man. We are born into it and belong to it. We are subject to the common laws of human nature, and we submit to them with good or ill grace. It does not mean very much to us. But suppose we come to understand that this race of man to which we belong, is bound together by something deeper and more vital than subjection to an outward law, that there is a vicarious element in human life, that no man liveth to himself and no man dieth to himself, that all the efforts and aspirations and toils and sufferings of humanity serve us and are for our sake. This is true in the plainest and most literal sense. The houses that shelter us, the clothes that cover us, the food on our tables, have all been won for us by the labour of other hands. We have paid for that labour, it is true, but there is one thing that we have not paid for, and that is the life that has gone into the labour.

And there is another thing that has been done for some of us — for all of us in this congregation in some measure — that we have not paid for and cannot repay. I mean the subjection of great multitudes of our fellow-creatures to hard and narrow and oppressive conditions of life, to poverty and to dull, distasteful toil, in order that we should be free to follow the callings which are, I will not say higher, but certainly cleaner and brighter and more beautiful, in order that we should have the means and the time for culture and refinement and an expanded life. I am not concerned now to explain or justify this state of things. I am taking it simply as a fact, and I say that the true nobility of our human sentiment can only come from a sense of the meaning of that fact. When we realize that every liberty, every privilege, every advantage, that comes to us as men and women has been bought with a price, — that the dark, subterranean lives of those who toil day and night in the bowels of the earth, the perils and hardships of those who sail to and fro upon the stormy seas, the benumbing weariness of those who dig and ditch and handle dirt, the endless tending of looms and plying of needles and carrying of burdens, —

> " the fierce confederate storm
> Of sorrow barricadoed evermore
> Within the walls of cities," —

all this is done and endured and suffered by our fellow-men, though blindly, for our benefit, and accrues to our advantage, — when we begin to understand this, a nobler spirit enters into us, the only spirit that can keep our wealth, our freedom, our culture from being a curse to us forever, and sinking us into the *ennui* of a selfish hell.

Noblesse oblige, — that is the true motto of a nobility worthy of the name. The higher the elevation, the deeper and wider is the obligation. The ideal of kingship is not to be found in the luxurious and licentious palace of the Shah of Persia, but in the hospitals of Naples, where the King of Italy bends to help and comfort the poorest of his subjects. Every touch of beauty, of light, of power, every gift of riches, of freedom, of learning that is ours, has been paid for by the lives of our fellow-men, and binds us to their service. It is this thought alone which can reveal to us the immense meaning of humanity, and fit us for our part in life, and make us truly noble men and gentle women. We are bought with a price.

And now some of you may ask why I have dwelt so long upon these propositions in regard to human life and said nothing yet about religion, made no direct comment upon the text. This is the reason. It is because life is part of religion, and religion is part of life. It is because the great truth of redemption by Jesus Christ is not a strange, unnatural, unreasonable, inhuman truth, but profoundly natural and reasonable, and fitted in, by a divine adaptation, to the very inmost recesses of our human nature. It is because the beauty and power of the text come not from the fact that it is foreign to our experience, — a mystic and incomprehensible word, — but rather from the fact that it is cognate to our experience. Everything fine and pure and uplifting in our life points to it and throws light upon it.

Our physical, intellectual, and social happiness depends on our belonging to something greater than ourselves. How, then, shall we find our spiritual happiness, save in belonging to God? Our deliverance from the lower servitude of life comes through the knowledge of its higher and wider allegiance. How, then, shall we be freed from the slavery of sin and self and sense and death, save by coming into subjection to God? The inspiration of the service that we render in this world to our homes, our country, our fellow-men, springs from the recognition that a price has been paid for us; the vital power of noble conduct rises from the deep fountain of gratitude, which flows not with water, but with warm heart's-blood. How then, shall a like power come into our religion, how shall it be as real, as living, as intimate, as our dearest human tie, unless we know and feel that God has paid a price for us, that He has bought us with his own precious life?

And this is the truth which the Gospel reveals to us. This is the price of which the text speaks; it is the incarnation, life, sufferings and death of the Son of God. This is the great ransom which has been given for all. He gave himself to poverty, to toil, to humiliation, to agony, to the cross. He gave himself for us, not only for our benefit, but in our place. He bore the trials and temptations which belong to us. He carried our sins. He endured our punishment. Through torture and anguish He went down to our death. Through loneliness and sorrow He descended into our grave. If it were merely a human being who had done this for us, it would be much. But since it was a Divine Being, it is infinitely more precious. Think of the almighty One becoming weak, the glorious One suffering shame, the holy One dwelling amongst sinners, the very Son of God pouring out his blood for us upon the accursed tree! It is this divinity in the sacrifice that gives it power to reconcile and bind our hearts to God. It is God himself proving how much He loves us by the price which He is willing to pay for us. It is God himself manifest in the flesh to redeem us from sin and death, in order that we may belong to Him entirely and forever.

Words fail me to express the splendour and might of this great truth as it is revealed in the Holy Scriptures. It is the wisdom of God and the power of God unto salvation. It is the supreme revelation of the Divine nature, which is like the human nature, and yet so far outshines it as the sun outshines a taper. It tells us what God will do for us; for "He that spared not his own Son, but freely delivered Him up for us, how shall He not also, with Him, freely give us all things?" It tells us what we owe to God: "for He died for all, that they which live should not henceforth live unto themselves, but unto Him which died for them and rose again." It is the source and centre of a true theology. It is the spring and motive of a high morality. It is the secret of a new life, redeemed, consecrated, sanctified by the Son of God, who loved us and gave himself for us.

A great deal of our religious thought and teaching to-day is turned to the example of Christ as the model and pattern of true manhood. And we rejoice in this, because it is a high and noble doctrine. But let us not forget that if it stands alone it is partial and incomplete. The force of an example, however lofty, has its limits. The life of Christ as an ideal falls short of the power to save us and uplift us, unless it is also a ransom, a life freely given and sacrificed for us. If

He were our example only, his very elevation above us, the purity and splendour of his character, the perfection of his moral triumph compared with our feeble and sinful lives, would discourage and cast us down. As well ask a common man to show the genius of a Dante or a Shakespeare, to exercise the power of a Cæsar or a Charlemagne, as to live the life of Christianity with nothing but an example to guide and bind us. But because that life is something more, because it is given and sacrificed for us, it becomes a vital and spiritual power, it lays hold of us at the very centre of our being. While it covers our sins and shortcomings, it awakens our noblest longings and desires. It sets us free to follow it, and to follow it to success.

Man will never grow beyond the need of that ransom. For all other ways of finding peace with God, of making sure that He loves us, of entering into the sense of forgiveness and fellowship with Him, are vain and futile compared with the Divine sacrifice. Peace through the cross alone, is true for us as it was for Paul. Man will never grow beyond the power of that great ransom to test and judge his soul, to reveal the thoughts of his heart, to prove whether he will be saved or lost. For here is the solemn mystery of it all, that, though this price was paid for every man, yet every man is free to appropriate or to reject the gift, to acknowledge or deny the obligation. And those who do not feel its preciousness and its binding power, those who count the blood of the covenant wherewith they were redeemed a common thing, and deny the Lord that bought them, are beyond the reach of any ransom. God himself is to them as " a stranger and as a man astonished, a mighty man that cannot save."

And so, my friends, I have set the truth before you by which the course of all your years, stretching far on beyond this life, must be determined. I point you to the Saviour, who alone can set you free from the curse of sin, from the bondage of the law, from the fear of death, by bringing you into his love and service. You are bought with a price. Christ has come and borne your burdens with you, and your sins for you. Henceforth there is not one of you that need be anxious about the forgiveness of your sins, the salvation of your souls. It is all purchased and paid for, if you will accept it. But with it YOU ARE PURCHASED, and you belong to the Lord Christ. " He has conquered sin, so that you need not be its slave any longer. Now let Him conquer you by his great love, and so his victory will be complete."

We desire our life to be a life of freedom, a life of noble service, a life of glad and happy labour for that which is highest and best. There is only one way to make it so, and that is to live it under the controlling power of the great price that has been paid for us. Acknowledge the Lord Jesus as your Saviour, Owner, Master, King. Confess the greatness of your obligation to Him. Confess that you can never repay it. And then give yourself to Him to live as bravely, as purely, as faithfully, as nobly as you can in his name and for his sake.

> " Were the whole realm of nature mine,
>   That were a present far too small:
> Love so amazing, so divine,
>   Demands my life, my soul, my all."

VI

ABRAHAM'S ADVENTURE

"And he went out, not knowing whither he went."
Hebrews xi. 8.

'**And he went out, not knowing whither he went.**"

THIS text describes a life of adventure. It brings before us one of that noble company of explorers who forsake the beaten track and push out into a new, strange, uncertain course for the sake of discovering and possessing a new world.

These men always appear heroic. There is something in them which compels our admiration. There is something in us which responds to their daring, and follows their journeyings with eager interest. I suppose it is the old, migratory instinct, — the instinct which first drew the tribes of men out from their original homes, and peopled the distant regions of the earth, — it is this deep, curious impulse of wandering and discovery which still lingers in our nature, and stirs us with strange thrills of enthusiasm, and fills us with wild day-dreams of adventure as we read or hear the story of some famous traveller in unknown lands. There is an explorer latent in almost every man whose mind is large enough to have any interests outside of himself; and it is this unused and frustrated explorer who sits beside the fire and pores, entranced and fascinated, over the Arctic diaries of Dr. Kane or the African journals of Stanley. He recognizes and applauds the heroism of these men, who went out, not knowing whither they went.

The power which has moved adventurers is faith. This is the vital force of almost all the great explorers. They have not gone forth vaguely and aimlessly to wander to and fro upon the face of the earth. They have believed in something unseen, something that other men have not believed in, something that has seemed to the world impossible and absurd, and they have set forth to seek it. A new continent across the ocean, a new passage from sea to sea, a new lake among the forests, a new land to be possessed and cultivated, a goal beyond sight and beyond knowledge, apprehended and realized by a heroic faith, has drawn them over stormy seas and inhospitable deserts, through rugged mountains and trackless jungles. They have believed, and therefore adventured.

Nor has their faith been lacking, for the most part, in a spiritual element. There is hardly one of them — not one, I think, among the very greatest of the world's explorers — who has not believed in God, and in his overruling Providence, and in his call to them to undertake their adventures. It is wonderful and beautiful to see how this religious element has entered into the exploration of the earth, and how faith has asserted itself in the most famous and glorious journeyings of men. We see Columbus planting the standard of the cross on the lonely beach of San Salvador; and Balboa kneeling silent, with uplifted hands, on the cliff from which he first caught sight of the Pacific; 'and Livingstone praying in his tent in the heart of Africa. From all the best and the bravest adventurers we hear the confession that they are the servants of a Divine Being, summoned and sent by Him to a work for which they would give Him the glory.

Now the life of Abraham takes an honourable place in the history of adventure for several reasons. It seems to me that its antiquity and originality entitle it to respect. But apart from this, in itself Abraham's adventure was momentous and significant. Other enterprises may appear to us more important and eventful than his; but, after all, it may be doubted whether any expedition that man has ever undertaken has had larger results in the history of the world than the emergence of the father of the Hebrew race from Mesopotamian bondage. Other journeys may seem to us more striking and wonderful than his pilgrimage from Ur of the Chaldees to the land of Caanan; but if we knew the story of its hardships and perils, if we understood the complex civilization which he forsook and the barbarism which he faced, we might not think it unworthy to be compared with the most famous travels. But the one thing in this ancient story which has survived the oblivion of the centuries, the one thing which shines out in it clear and distinct, and makes it glorious and precious beyond comparison, is its imperishable and unalterable testimony to the power of faith to make a brave man face the unknown.

Abraham believed. He lived in an idolatrous country. Every one about him, even his own father and his family, worshipped idols. But Abraham's soul pierced through all these falsehoods and delusions of men to find and clasp the one living and true God who is a Spirit.

Abraham believed. He was surrounded by the unrighteousness that a corrupt religion always sanctions and intensifies. The pollutions and cruelties of heathen life touched him on every side, and must have left their stain upon him. He himself was far from righteous. There were flaws in his character, blots upon his conduct. But one thing he did not do. He did not carve an idol out of his own sin and call it a God. He believed in a God who was not lower but higher than himself, — a God of purity, of holiness, of truth, of mercy; and that faith, having in itself the power to uplift and purify, was counted to him for righteousness, — yea, it was better than any outward conformity to a code of morality, just as religion is better than ethics, because it has the promise of growth and enlargement and an endless life.

Abraham believed. He was bound by the ties of the world, of habit, of social order, of self-interest, — by all those delicate and innumerable threads which seem to fasten a man to the ground, as the Lilliputians fastened Gulliver, and make liberty of thought, of belief, of conduct impossible. But in the midst of his bondage Abraham heard the voice of the God who had a message, a mission, a call for his soul, — a message which meant spiritual freedom, a mission which could only be fulfilled by obedience, a call which said, "Get thee out of thy country, and from thy kindred, and from thy father's house, unto the land that I will show thee." Think what that involved, — separation from the past, resignation of all his customs and plans of life, the entrance upon an untrodden path, the following of an unseen and absolute guidance, the consecration of his life to a journey through strange lands, among strange people, towards a strange goal, — the final and supreme adventure of his soul. But Abraham obeyed the call. "He went out, not knowing whither he went." And that was faith.

Let us think for a little while of this aspect of faith. It is an adventure. It is a going out into the unknown future under the guidance of God.

I. All faith recognizes that life is a pilgrimage whose course and duration cannot be foreseen. That is true, indeed, whether we acknowledge it or not. Even if a man should fancy that his existence was secure, and that he could direct his own career and predict his own future, experience would teach him his mistake. But the point is that faith recognizes this uncertainty of life at the outset, and in a peculiar way, which transforms it from a curse into a blessing and makes it possible for us even to be glad that we must "go out not knowing whither we go."

For what is it that faith does with these lives of ours? It just takes them up out of our weak, trembling, uncertain control and puts them into the hands of God. It makes them a part of his great plan. It binds them fast to his pure and loving will, and fills them with his life. Unless we believe that God has made us and made us for himself, unless we believe that He has something for each one of us to do and to be, unless we believe that He knows what our life's way should be and has marked it out for us, how is it possible for us to go forward with cheerful confidence? But if we do believe this, then of course we shall be willing to accept our own ignorance of the future, and, so far from hindering us in our advance, it will encourage and strengthen us to remember that the meaning of our life is so large that we cannot understand it. It will not fit into our broken and imperfect knowledge just because it does fit perfectly into the great wisdom of God.

Do you see what I mean? The man who has no faith either accepts the uncertainty of life as a necessity of fate; he is caught in the net of a hidden destiny, which to him can never seem anything else than a blind chance, because there is no purpose and no law in it, — or else he fights against the uncertainty of life, and tries to conquer it by his own skill and prudence and pertinacity. He chooses the object of his ambition, and the line of conduct which shall lead him to it; he marks out a career for himself, and pushes forward to fulfil it according to his own plan. And then every event that crosses his plan is a cause of anxiety and irritation; every call of duty that lies outside of it is an interruption and a burden; every change that comes to him is a disappointment and a defeat; every delay in the accomplishment of his schemes frets him to the heart; and when disaster and sickness and death come near to him he trembles, for he knows that they may easily wreck and destroy his life. He means to be a self-made man; he will supply the material and construct the model; he assures himself that he knows what the result will be. But all the time he is working among forces which may shatter him and his plan in a moment. Even while he dreams of success he stands face to face with failure. It seems to me that must make life a feverish and fitful thing; a long, weary, continual anxiety of heart.

But the man who has faith accepts the uncertainty of life as the consequence of its larger significance; he cannot interpret it, because it means so much; he cannot trace its lines through to the end, because it has no end, it runs on into God's eternity. Something better is coming into it than worldly success. Something better is coming out of it than wealth or fame or power. He is not making himself. God is making him, and that after a model which eye hath not seen, but which is to be manifest in the consummation of the sons of God. So he can toil away at his work, not knowing whether he is to see its result now or not, but knowing that God will not let it be wasted. So he can run with patience the race that is set before him, not knowing whether he shall come in first or last among his fellows, but knowing that his prize is secure. So he can labour at the edifice of his life, not knowing whether it is to be finished according to his plans or not, but knowing that it surely will be completed, and surely will find its place in the great temple which God is building. Thus his uncertainty becomes the ground of his certainty. Failure, disaster, ruin are impossible for him. Change may come to him as it comes to other men, but it does not mean calamity. Disappointment he may have to meet as other men meet it, but it cannot bring despair. Death will surely find him, and he cannot tell when it will come; but he knows that it will not come before the time; it will not break his life off in the middle, but will finish one part of it and begin another. Loss, final and irretrievable loss, — no, the man who believes never can be lost, because he willingly goes forth not knowing whither he goes, with God for his leader and guide.

II. This, then, is the broadest meaning of faith's adventure: it is the surrender of life to a hidden guidance. And bound up together with this, as an essential part of it, we find the necessity that faith should accept the religious life as an adventure full of unknown trials and tests and temptations. No one can tell beforehand just how many hardships he must pass through, just how many sacrifices he must make, just how many assaults of evil he must resist, if he sets out to walk with God.

Abraham did not know what would meet him on his life-long journey: the day of peril in Egypt when he would break down and disgrace himself; the day of dissension with Lot when he would prove his fidelity and his love; the days of conflict with the Rephaim and the Zuzim and the Emim and the Horites, when he would overthrow them; the day of temptation when the king of Sodom would offer to make him rich; the day of sharpest sorrow when he would be called to show his supreme devotion by resigning his beloved son into the hands of the Lord, — all these days were hidden from him as he entered upon the long journey. All that God required of him was that he would meet them as they came; not beforehand, in imagination, in promise and definite resolution, but at the appointed hour, in the crisis of trial: then, and not till then, Abraham must face his conflict, and make his sacrifice, and hold fast his faith.

Not otherwise does God deal with us. He does not show us exactly what it will cost to obey Him. He asks us only to give what He calls for from day to day. Here is one sacrifice right in front of us that we must make now in order to serve God, — some evil habit to be given up, some lust of the flesh to be crucified and slain; and that is our trial for to-day. But to-morrow that trial may be changed from a hardship into a blessing, it may become a joy and triumph to us; and another trial, new, different, unforeseen, may meet us in the way. Now, perhaps, it is poverty that you have to endure, fighting with its temptations to envy and discontent, and general rebellion against the order of the world; ten years hence, it may be wealth that will test you with its temptations to pride, and luxury, and self-reliance, and general arrogance toward your fellowmen. Now, it may be some selfish indulgence that you have to resign; to-morrow, it may be some one whom you love, from whom you must consent to part at the call of God. To-day, it may be your ease, your comfort, your indolence that you must sacrifice for the sake of doing good in the world; to-morrow, it may be your activity, your energy, the work you delight in, that you must give up while sickness lays its heavy hand upon you, and bids you "stand and wait." To-day one thing, to-morrow another thing; and God does not tell you what it will be: He calls you to go out into your adventure not knowing whither you go.

It is this very indefiniteness of the Christian life that frightens unbelief and allures faith. It is this very necessity of facing the unknown that divides between doubting and believing souls. If we doubt the power and the love of God, if we doubt the grace and the truth of Christ, we will hesitate and hold back. We will demand to know all about the way before we enter upon it. "How much must we give up, what sacrifices must we make, how shall we ever be able to meet the trials and temptations of the future? No, we cannot go out after Christ, because we do not know where He will lead us and how hard it may be to follow."

But if we believe that this God is our God, and will be our guide even unto death, if we believe that this Christ is our only Saviour and Master, our Divine Leader and Guide, then we can go after Him the more gladly just because He does not tell us all at once what we must resign and suffer and resist for his sake. That, indeed, might crush and dishearten us; for if we knew all at once, we could not help trying our strength against it all. But since we know only to-day's temptation, to-day's trial, to-day's conflict, to-day's cross, to-day; since we know that He who ordered it is with us and will help us to bear it,—we can follow Him in confidence.

"We know not what the path may be
　　As yet by us untrod;
But we can trust our all to thee,
　　Our Father and our God.

"If called like Abram's child to climb
　　The hill of sacrifice,
Some angel may be there in time,
　　Deliverance may arise.

"Or if some darker lot be good,
　　Oh teach us to endure
The sorrow, pain, or solitude,
　　That makes the spirit pure."

III. Once more, the adventure of faith involves the going out to meet unknown duties and to perform hidden tasks.

In one sense the scheme and outline of a religious life are clear and distinct beforehand; the principles of faith and hope and love by which it is to be guided, the laws of righteousness and truth and mercy by which it is to be governed, are fixed and unchangeable, the same always and for all men. But in another sense the religious life has no scheme and outline at all. Its responsibilities, its opportunities, its labours arise from day to day. One man has one thing to do; another man has another thing to do. The duty of the present may be changed, enlarged, transformed in the future.

See how this is brought out in the life of Abraham. At first he has only to bear witness to the true God among an idolatrous people; and then he has to set out on a perilous journey towards Canaan; and then he has to take care of his flocks and herds in the wilderness; and then he has to deliver his kinsman Lot from the sword of the tyrant Chedorlaomer; and then he has to exercise hospitality towards the angels of God. Abraham's duty is not written down and delivered to him at the beginning. It is kept secret from him, and he goes out to meet it, not knowing what it will be.

That is the law of the life of faith. The man who takes a principle into his heart commits himself to an uncertainty, he enters upon an adventure. He must be ready for unexpected calls and new responsibilities.

The Samaritan who rode down from Jerusalem to Jericho had nothing to do in the morning but follow that highway, and take care that his beast did not stumble or hurt itself, or get tired out so that it could not finish the journey. He was just a solitary horseman, and all that he needed to do was to have a good seat in the saddle and a light hand on the bit. But at noon, when he came to the place where that unknown pilgrim lay senseless and bleeding beside the road, — then, in a moment, the Samaritan's duty changed, and God called him to be a rescuer, a nurse, a helper of the wounded.

Peter, when he rested on the housetop in Joppa, was only a pastor of the Jewish Christian church; his mission was to instruct and guide his kinsmen according to the flesh. But when the great vision of a catholic church flashed upon him, when the knocking of the messengers of the Roman centurion sounded up from the gate of the courtyard, then, in a moment, Peter's duty was changed, and he was called to go to the house of a Gentile and proclaim the gospel of Christ without respect of persons. Read the lives of the heroes of faith, and you will find that they are all like this. They set out to perform, not one task only, but anything that God may command. They accept Christ's commission, and set sail upon an unknown ocean with sealed orders.

That takes courage. It is a risk, a venture. But for the spiritual as truly as for the temporal life the rule is, "Nothing venture, nothing win." And is it not infinitely nobler and more inspiring to enter upon a career like that, — a career which is to run so close to God that He can speak into it and fill it with new meanings, new possibilities, new tasks, at any moment, — is not that infinitely finer and more glorious than to make a contract to do a certain thing for a certain price, as if God were a manufacturer and we were his mill-hands? It seems to me that this is the very proof and bond of friendship with Him, this calling of faith to an unlimited and undefined obedience. If we will accept it, it will send us forward on a life that grows and expands and unfolds itself, and wins new powers and capacities, as it girds itself to meet the new duties that lie hidden in the future. It will not be a dull and dry routine: it will be an enterprise, a voyage of discovery, an exploration of the divine possibilities of living. And the joy of it, the enthusiasm and inspiration of it, will not be the tame thought that nothing more can be required of us than what we already see, but the strong assurance that power will be given to us for every task that our Master sets. "Follow me," He cried, "and I will make you fishers of men." How and when and where they should labour the disciples knew not. They knew only that He would fit them for their duty when it met them. Even so He speaks to us. And even so we must follow Him into the unknown future, answering his call in the noble words of St. Augustine: "Lord, give what thou commandest, and command what thou wilt."

IV. Only one word remains to be added. Faith is an adventure; it is the courage of the soul to face the unknown. But that courage springs from the hope and confidence of the soul that its adventure will succeed. Beyond the unknown, beyond the uncertainties and perils and responsibilities of the earthly future, it sees the certain, the secure, the imperishable, — "an inheritance incorruptible and undefiled and that fadeth not away, reserved in heaven for you, who are kept by the power of God through faith unto salvation, ready to be revealed in the last time."

How grandly that certainty of faith comes

out in the story of Abraham! A pilgrim and a stranger, a man without a country, wandering up and down between the lands of Egypt and Chaldea, involved in strange conflicts and unexpected trials, his white tent shining in the sunlight and shaking in the wind, as it rested here and there among the highland pastures and on the steep hills of Caanan, for a hundred years, a sojourner in the land of promise as in a land not his own, — yet that noble old father of the faithful, that loyal friend and follower of God, was never an aimless man, never an uncertain man, never a hopeless man. He went forth not knowing whither he went, but he also looked for "a city that hath foundations, whose builder and maker is God."

Sublime assurance, glorious pilgrimage! And is not that the type and symbol of the life of faith? Of the nearer future, the future that lies among the mountains and valleys, the pastures and deserts of this world, it is ignorant, and yet it does not fear to face it; for it sees that the final future, the blessed rest and reward of the soul that serves and follows its Divine Master, is secure. It knows whither Christ has gone, and it knows the hidden way. And along that way it presses steadily to its goal of everlasting peace.

> " On through waste and blackness,
>   O'er our desert road ;
> On till Sinai greet us,
>   Mountain of our God!
> On past Edom's valley,
>   Moab's mountain wall,
> Jordan's seaboard rushings,
>   The pillar cloud o'er all!
> Past the palmy city,
>   Rock and hill our road,
> On till Salem greet us,
>   City of our God! "

VII

SOLOMON'S CHOICE

"Give me now wisdom and knowledge, that I may go out and come in before this people: for who can judge this thy people that is so great?"

2 *Chronicles* i. 10.

"Give me now wisdom and knowledge."

THESE words were spoken by Solomon, the greatest, wisest, and in some respects the meanest of the Hebrew kings. His life is one of the standing riddles of history. Never man began so fairly and ended so darkly. The blossoms of his youth were like the flowers on the tree of life: the fruits of his old age were like Dead Sea apples, full of dust. In him genius was wedded to sin, and success was the mother of failure. Bright as was the promise of his early years, glorious as were the achievements of his manhood, the clouds that gathered round his death were so heavy and dark that men have remained in doubt whether his final place is among the saved or among the lost. The fathers of the church held opposite opinions on the subject; and in Pietro Lorenzetti's great fresco of the resurrection, in the Campo Santo at Pisa, the uncertainty of Solomon's fate is represented by the painter, who has placed him in the middle of the picture, looking doubtfully around, not knowing whether he is to be called to the right hand or to the left. Perhaps, after all, the painter was prudent, for the question of final destiny is one which we can never solve in regard to any human being. Wise and simple, beggar and king, as they pass from our sight, we must leave them to the justice and mercy of the omniscient God.

But the questions of character and conduct as they arise here in this world are within the reach of our understanding, and it is to a study of some of these questions as they are suggested by the life of Solomon that I invite your attention now. The history of his life is illustrated in three great visions which came to him at three successive periods of his strange career. Three times God visited him in the night watches; three times the curtain which hides the future was lifted, and the darkness of his sleep was illumined with the secret flash of truth.

The first vision came at the beginning of his career, when the untried course of life was just opening before him. It contained a glorious promise and a solemn warning. It revealed the elements of strength and the elements of weakness in one of the most marvellous characters the world has ever seen. The Lord appeared to him in Gibeon and said, "Ask what I shall give thee." Solomon's answer was in the words of the text.

The second vision came to him at the very climax of his splendour and power, when the great temple, which was the central spot of glory in his land and in his reign, was completed and dedicated. When the echoes of rejoicing had died away in the royal city, and the people were returning with gladness to their tents, then the Lord appeared to Solomon the second time, as He had appeared unto him at Gibeon. The awful voice, sounding in the silence of the king's heart, declared that the prayer of dedication had been heard. The temple was accepted and blessed. God would make his dwelling there perpetually. "But if ye shall at all turn from following me, ye or your children, and will not keep my commandments and my statutes which I have set before you, but go and serve other gods, and worship them; then will I cut off Israel out of the land which I have given them; and this house, which I have hallowed for my name, will I cast out of my sight; and Israel shall be a proverb and a byword among all nations."

The third vision came to the king in the decline and shame of his old age, when the evils against which he had been warned had come upon him, when his heart had been entangled with strange women and stranger gods, when the misused wealth and perverted power which had been his were turning to dross and corruption within his hands. Then God was angry with him, and appeared to him once more and said: "Forasmuch as this is done of thee, and thou hast not kept my covenant and my statutes which I have commanded thee, I will surely rend the kingdom from thee, and will give it to thy servant. Notwithstanding in thy days I will not do it, for David thy father's sake: but I will rend it out of the hand of thy son." A dreadful dream, stern, angry, terrible: the only gleam of mercy in it was shown, not for Solomon's sake, but for the sake of his dead father, who was dear to God; a vision of dishonour and darkness and swift-coming disaster closing with black wings about the declining days of him who had once been the brightest and most prosperous and best beloved of Israel's monarchs. What is the meaning of it? How shall we explain it? How shall we read and understand its lesson? How is it possible that a dream so bright and fair as that which crowned his youth should turn into a dream so black and shameful as that which shadowed his old age?

It is to solve this mystery that I ask you to turn back again to the opening vision of Solomon's life. Scrutinize it more closely, study it more deeply. See if you cannot discern in it the fatal flaw which marred the character of the royal philosopher, and through which at last his life was brought to ruin.

The circumstances of Solomon at the time of this first and most famous dream are worthy of our careful attention. He was, as you know, the youngest son of King David, who by his strong and heroic qualities, under the blessing of God, had brought the kingdom to a state of prosperity and power. The sovereignty of Israel at the close of David's long and warlike reign was something vastly richer and grander and more potent than it was when the big, blundering Saul was chosen king; and the sceptre which David held in his weary and trembling hand was the symbol of a wide and successful dominion over a turbulent but mighty people. To whom should he leave it? His two oldest sons, Absalom and Ammon, had proved unworthy, and were dead. The old king's heart turned now to his last-born child, the darling of his declining years, and to him he gave the kingdom, calling him Solomon, "the peaceful one," and centring all the hope and love of his heart upon the happiness and prosperity of this chosen son.

How strange it is, and yet how common, for the father to desire a character and destiny for his son different from his own! The man of war desires his heir to be a man of peace. And how strange also, and yet how nearly inevitable, that the father's sins should entwine themselves with the life of the child that he loves best!

The mother of Solomon was Bathsheba, a woman of great beauty, but of whose moral character the less said the better, for she was certainly the occasion, and I cannot help feeling that she was at least passively the cause, of her husband's death and her monarch's crime; and she was the only one who profited by the whole shameful history, for it raised her not unwillingly from the wife of a common man to the wife of a king. "Now in Eastern lands and under a system of polygamy," says a wise observer, "the son is more dependent even than elsewhere upon the character of the mother." And I believe that Solomon's whole life felt the influence of such a mother. Ambitious but comfort-loving, passionate but cold, inwardly sensual but outwardly devout, fascinating but intensely selfish, she was one of those whom Goethe called "problematic characters," who attain the greatest external success, but are forever unhappy and unsatisfied because they never lose or forget themselves. And from her, by birth and education, Solomon received the qualities which were brought out in his after-life.

He was admirably fitted to rule, trained in all the requirements of royalty, inspired with a sense of the dignity and responsibility of his position, every inch a king; but he was never taught to escape from his greatest foe and final destroyer, himself; and thus his noblest actions and his greatest successes were turned into failures.

But we are running before our history. Let us turn back to regard Solomon, the young king, not yet twenty years of age, seated on the throne of his father, the inheritor of a dominion among the most splendid of the Eastern world. He desires to inaugurate his reign with an act of religious worship, for this is eminently proper, and in no other way will his royal magnificence be seen to better advantage. God has forbidden the people to offer sacrifice in the high places on the mountain-tops, but custom has sanctioned the violation of this command, and Solomon cares more for the popular usage and for a grand display than for a forgotten and obsolete law. He goes with a solemn procession to the top of Mt. Gibeon, where stands the great brazen altar of Bezaleel, and there he offers a thousand burnt-offerings, filling the whole heavens with the smoke of his kingly sacrifices and the noise of his royal worship.

The smoke rolls away. The last echoes of the solemn music die among the hills. Solomon is asleep in his tent on the mountain. And now comes that wondrous dream which foreshadows the course of his whole life. God appears to him, and asks him to choose that which he desires more than all things else. Solomon chooses " wisdom and knowledge to go out and come in before the people." God approves the choice and promises to add wealth and honour. Solomon awakes and the dream is true ; but, for all that, he dies in sin and sorrow and dishonour. How shall we explain the mystery?

Three questions, it seems to me, will go to the root of the matter : —

Why did God approve of Solomon's choice, and yet not approve of him?

Why was Solomon the wisest of men, and yet one of the greatest of fools?

Why did Solomon have all that he desired, and yet remain forever unsatisfied?

I. God approved of Solomon's choice because it was relatively right. As between wealth and fame and wisdom, the young king instantly and instinctively seized the greatest and noblest of the three. Wisdom is more than riches or fame, because it is the fountain of both. An understanding heart, the ability to discriminate between the good and the bad among men and causes and enterprises, is certainly the most valuable possession for every man, especially for one who is called to rule over his fellows. For without this, the richest and most powerful potentate will come to nought. How strange that men, even from the standpoint of this world, do not understand this! They crave wealth, not thinking that wealth in the hands of a fool only makes him a prey to knaves. They aspire to power, not remembering that power in the hands of one who is not wise enough for it only makes him a laughing-stock. How many a weak brother, who might have lived respected in obscurity, has become ridiculous by the sudden gift of riches or office! Wisdom is the principal thing, for if a man has that he can acquire and use the others. And Solomon's magnificence, the prosperity of his kingdom, and the fame of his reign all came from his gift of wisdom, so wisely chosen.

But although this choice was relatively right, it was not absolutely the best. There was something better for which he might have asked, and which, if he had received it, would have brought down the blessing of God not only upon his reign, but upon his own soul forever.

What was the burden of David's prayers before God? What was the deep and burning desire of David's heart, not only in his youth, but also in his old age, growing and deepening as it was answered and fed by God? It was the longing for holiness, the consuming hunger and thirst after righteousness, which is the noblest pain and the richest want of the soul. Blessed are they who feel it, for they shall be filled. "Create in me a clean heart, O God, and renew a right spirit within me." This was David's prayer, the highest and the best: not first an understanding heart, but first a clean heart, cleansed by the Divine pardon from the stains of guilt, and freed by the Divine power from the defilement of sin. He felt the burden of iniquity, the shame and sorrow of uncleanness, the slavery of self, and he cried to be delivered. If God would grant him this, it would be more to him than all beside. "Purge me with hyssop and I shall be clean; wash me and I shall be whiter than snow."

This is the noblest choice. Wisdom is good, but holiness is as far above wisdom as Christ is above Socrates. If Solomon had only been wise enough to choose this, if he had only felt his greatest weakness and his deepest need, and asked for a pure and holy heart, how rich beyond expression would have been the results of that vision, — rich not only for this world, but for that which is to come: rich in the approval of the living God; rich in the salvation of his immortal soul; rich in an entrance into that heavenly kingdom which shall endure when all the thrones and crowns and sceptres of this world have crumbled into dust!

Let us remember that while these earthly kingdoms are founded upon wealth and power and wisdom, God's kingdom is founded on holiness of character. And though we may achieve greatness in these lower realms, though we may become merchant princes, or political rulers, or kings of thought, the least in the kingdom of heaven, yes, the simplest, poorest child who has known God's love and felt his purifying Spirit in the heart, will be greater than we are, so long as our sole inheritance is in the kingdoms of this world.

II. Why was Solomon the wisest of men, and yet one of the greatest of fools? In order to answer this question we must scrutinize his choice very closely. And if we do this we shall see that the wisdom for which he asked was peculiar and limited. It was political wisdom, such as befits a king and renders him able to rule successfully over the minds of men. He felt that the difficulties of governing his tumultuous and rebellious people would be almost insuperable unless he had a more than human insight into character, and tact in controlling men. And so he asked for wisdom and knowledge to go out and come in before the people.

Now, as a king, this was what he most needed. But Solomon was a man before he was a king. And, as a man, what he most needed was an understanding heart to guide his own life. Perhaps he thought he was wise enough for this already. Perhaps he thought he was able to rule his inner kingdom for himself, if God would only help him with the outer. And herein lay his folly, for a man can more easily control and guide the destinies of a great nation than he can bind and direct the passions of his own disordered and tumultuating heart.

It is easier to take a city than to rule your own spirit. History proves it in the lives of hundreds of great men who have been able to control the forces of politics, but not to guide their own lives, not to resist their own besetting sins of avarice or lust. It would be strange if we could not read this lesson in our own times in the dark, sad story of Rudolph, the crown-prince of Austria. Heir to one of the proudest thrones of Europe, brilliant in his natural gifts, and developed by education into a man of many accomplishments, skilled in art and letters, and qualified to adorn his lofty station with extraordinary success, he was driven by his own hot and untamed passions, in the prime of his young manhood, to a dishonourable death and a suicide's grave.

Solomon's fatal weakness was for wives. I do not suppose that we are to understand that he was a gross sensualist. He probably sought mental excitement and change in the organization of his great household. One of his chief objects was to increase his political influence by contracting alliances with the princesses of surrounding nations. He thought he could manage the women, but he was foolish, for of course the women managed him. And still he went on adding to his burdens and entanglements, every month bringing a new princess into the royal household, and every princess bringing a new god, until at length he had seven hundred wives and three hundred concubines, and I think we must agree that the last state of that man was worse than the first. Hated by his people for the heavy burdens of taxation which he was forced to lay upon them for the support of his costly household, turned hither and thither by wives who neither understood his wisdom nor cared for his greatness but only for his gold, worshipping at the shrines of a hundred gods in none of whom he believed, — what an old age is this! It is the very mockery of greatness, the supreme irony of fate, that the hoary head of the wisest of monarchs should be crowned by his own hands with the cap of the fool. And all this because he did not understand that to guide one's own life is a harder and more perilous task than to rule a kingdom, because he did not learn to pray with David, "Teach me thy way, O Lord, and lead me in a plain path; send out thy light and thy truth, let them lead me."

III. Let us ask, now, the third and last

question. Why did Solomon have all that he desired, and yet remain unhappy? The answer is simple and straightforward: because he never forgot or lost himself. He tried to be happy. That was the chief end and aim of his life, his own success, his own felicity. He did not seek it in a low and sensual way; not in coarse pleasures nor in trifling pursuits. Solomon was far too wise for that. But in a high and grand and royal way he sought for happiness. The delight of knowing and understanding all things, the joy of feeling that in him more wisdom was centred than in all men before or after, the pride of the most splendid temple and the most prosperous kingdom and the most beneficent reign, — thus he sought his happiness and thus he never found it; for it is a law of God that they who will be happy never shall be; never shall clasp the phantom after which they run so eagerly, never shall feel the deep sweet calm of a contented soul, never shall rest in perfect peace, until they cease their mad chase, forget and deny themselves, and are lost and absorbed in some noble and unselfish pursuit. Then, and then only, happiness comes, as the angels came to

Jesus in the desert, and in Gethsemane, when He had renounced all hope of joy.

"He that loseth his life shall find it." The words of the Master, who was wiser than Solomon, are true now as then. We cannot have happiness until we forget to seek for it. We cannot find peace until we enter the path of self-sacrificing usefulness. We cannot be delivered from this "vain expense of passions that forever ebb and flow," this wretched, torturing, unsatisfied, unsatisfying self, until we come to Jesus and give our lives to Him to be absorbed as his life was in loving obedience to God and loving service to our fellow-men.

Let us draw this lesson from Solomon's dream. If God says to us, in the bright promise of youth, "Ask what I shall give thee," let us make the best choice, and answer, "Give me grace to know thy Son, the Christ, and to grow like Him; for that is the true wisdom which leads to eternal life, and that is the true royalty which brings dominion over self, and that is the true happiness which flows unsought from fellowship with the Divine Life."

VIII

PETER'S MISTAKE

"And Peter answered and said to Jesus, Master, it is good for us to be here: and let us make three tabernacles; one for thee, and one for Moses, and one for Elias. For he wist not what to say."

2 *Chronicles* i. 10.

"And Peter answered and said to Jesus, Master, it is good for us to be here: and let us make three tabernacles: one for thee, and one for Moses, and one for Elias."

ALL of the apostles of our Lord Jesus Christ made mistakes, for they were all human. But the Apostle Peter seems to have been almost more human than the others, and so more liable to error. There is no possibility of taking him for a mythical character, a demigod, or a legendary hero. He is too much like ourselves. A vessel filled to the brim with water is apt to spill a little when it is shaken. Peter is so full of human nature that, whenever he is excited or agitated, it seems to overflow, and some word or deed comes out, which would be almost childish in its impulsiveness, if it were not for the virile force of the great strong heart behind it. The consequence of this is, that he is more often in trouble, more frequently rebuked and corrected, than any other of the disciples.

And yet we love the Apostle Peter. We cannot help it. He was a man, take him for all in all. The very impetuosity which so often led him into a false position was a quality which, under proper discipline and restraint, fitted him to become the chief of the apostles, and the leader of the aggressive work of the church. I would rather have a man who sometimes caught fire at the wrong time, than one so damp and flabby that you could never get a spark of enthusiasm out of him. A clock which sometimes goes too fast is better than one which never goes at all. And there was one thing of which you could be always sure with Peter, — he never would profess to love you while at heart he was indifferent or hostile to you. He never would put his arm over your shoulder and call you " dear brother " while he was secretly endeavouring to get hold of your money, or circulating vague reports to discredit your reputation or undermine your influence. You could rely on seeing the worst and the best of Peter at once. He had not much tact, but his stock of candour was large. And it seems to me that in all his errors, with one possible exception, there was a root of true and noble feeling.

You will observe, in regard to the particular mistake which we are now to consider, first, that Peter knew that it was a mistake; and, second, that he was not ashamed to say so, and to make record of it against himself. It is in order to bring out these two points that I have chosen the text from St. Mark's Gospel. It would have been just as easy to take it from St. Matthew or St. Luke, but not half so instructive. For that which we call the Gospel according to Mark is in reality the Gospel according to Peter. Mark himself had not been a personal hearer or companion of Christ, but he was the evangelist, the scribe — or, as Papias calls him, the interpreter — of Peter, attaching himself to the apostle as a disciple and friend, listening with eager attention to his remembrances of the life and teachings of the Lord Jesus and his intercourse with the twelve, and writing down these things with conscientious care in order that after Peter's death they might not be lost, but faithfully given to the church. In effect, therefore, it is Peter himself who tells us in the text what he said on the Mount of Transfiguration. It is Peter himself who recognizes the folly of it. It is Peter himself who explains it with the humble confession that he did not know what he was talking about, that he said it just for the sake of saying something, " for he wist not what to say."

How hard it is to make an acknowledgment like this, to confess that we have spoken without thinking, that we have talked nonsense! How many a man says a thing in haste or in heat, without fully understanding or half meaning it, and then, because he has said it, holds fast to it, and tries to defend it as if it were true! But how much wiser, how much more admirable and attractive, it is when a man has the grace to perceive and acknowledge his mistakes! It gives us assurance that he is capable of learning, of growing, of improving, so that his future will be better than his past; and, especially in an autobiography, it makes us feel that we are reading, not a cunningly devised fable of impossible excellence, but the story of a real life. It is difficult to exaggerate the sense of confidence which we feel towards this narrative when we hear Peter telling the story of his own foolish saying as one of the incidents of the scene.

"He wist not what to say;" he was so overwhelmed with wonder and awe, he was so carried out of himself, that he felt himself utterly unable to express his feelings. His thoughts were shaken from their balance by the rush of emotion, and he stammered out the first words that came to his tongue. Something very marvellous must have happened to cause this confusion of mind. Let us inquire what it was. Let us recall the events which immediately preceded Peter's mistake.

Surely we must feel, as we read the simple, graphic account which is given by the first three Gospels, that we also are like Peter, and know not what to say. The Transfiguration of Christ is one of those wonderfully beautiful things which seem to defy analysis or description. When we try to conjure up the scene, imagination fails, and fancy, dazzled by the radiance, folds her wings before her eyes and is lost in dreams. Vainly has the genius of poet and painter attempted to depict the soft glory of that event. The highest achievement even of a Raphael falls far short of the reality; and his great picture in the Vatican is in fact only a confession of the impotence of the loftiest art to rise to the level of the divine. But while the actual wonder — the burst of splendour which irradiated and transformed the body of our blessed Lord — must remain for us a bright, inexplicable mystery, there are many details connected with the event which we can study and bring out more clearly; and this will certainly help us to understand it better.

In the first place we ought to notice, what may have hitherto escaped our attention, the time and the circumstances of the event. It was not thrown by chance into the history of Christ, — a stray flash of glory falling without design into the darkness of his lowly life. There was a reason why it should come just then. There was a close connection between the Transfiguration and the events which preceded and followed it.

It was just one week after that memorable day at Cæsarea Philippi, when the noble impulsiveness of Peter had led him to make, before any of his brethren, that confession of faith which Christ said should be the foundation-rock of his church. "Thou art the Christ, the son of the living God," cried the strong-hearted apostle; and you remember the blessing which followed these words. But do you remember also what came after that? Do you remember that Jesus then began to teach his disciples "that the Son of man must suffer many things, and be rejected of the elders and of the chief priests and scribes, and be killed, and after three days rise again"? These were hard lessons for the disciples to learn, just at the moment when their faith in the Master was opening its first buds of promise. The gospels make no secret of the fact that they did not, would not, could not believe them. These were hard lessons, also, for Jesus to teach. The thought of his shameful rejection by his people, the cruel treachery of Judas, the gloom and anguish of the crucifixion, the bitter and inexplicable pangs of the atonement, pressed heavily upon his soul. They seemed to descend upon Him at this time with peculiar force and intensity, as a diffused mist thickens suddenly into an impenetrable cloud. And now began that long agony which culminated in the garden of Gethsemane. It was not easy for Christ to face shame and death. Not easier, but harder, infinitely harder, than it would have been for you and me.

The week that followed this announcement of his approaching crucifixion is passed over in silence by the gospels. But we can easily believe that it was spent by Christ in close and loving intercourse with his disciples, trying to familiarize them with this sorrowful thought. And then, one evening, when the sun was sinking in the western sky and the cool hush of twilight was falling upon the weary world, He separated himself from the larger company, and taking with Him the three men who were nearest to his human heart, — the three who had most need and most fitness for such a revelation as was coming, — He went up into a high mountain to pray. He wished seclusion, but not solitude. He shrank from the pressure of the crowd, but not from the society of those whom He loved.

I think there is something profoundly touching in this trait of Jesus' character, — that He always, in every experience of the highest joy or the deepest sorrow, in the death-chamber of Jairus' daughter, at the grave of Lazarus, in the garden of Gethsemane, and on the Mount of Transfiguration, wished to have within call of his voice, and within reach of his hand, some friend whom He knew and trusted, some one who could give Him the sense of human sympathy. That is a chilly and frost-bound disposition which prefers to enjoy its happiness or bear its grief alone. The presence of a friend who can feel with us, even though imperfectly, the mere silent presence of a friend, even though he be asleep, as the friends of Jesus were, is something which enhances pleasure and mitigates sorrow in every true and noble heart.

It has long been a tradition of the church that the scene of the Transfiguration was Mount Tabor. But this has now been generally abandoned, because the summit of that hill was then occupied by a fortified city, and would not have afforded the seclusion which Jesus sought. It seems to be agreed among scholars that the high mountain which He ascended was one of the long ridges of Mount Hermon, that grand snow-clad barrier which stands between the Holy Land and the country of the Gentiles, and from whose slopes the pilgrim gains the most magnificent prospect over Galilee and Samaria, even to Jerusalem and the hills beyond it. The glories of a mountain sunset are the same to-day as they were eighteen centuries ago, and so we can gather from the descriptions of recent travellers a picture of the very scene which was spread before the eyes of Jesus and his disciples, as they climbed the mountain together.

A deep ruby flush came over the landscape, and warm purple shadows crept slowly down the valleys. The Sea of Galilee was lit up with a delicate greenish-yellow hue between its dim mountain walls. Then the flush faded, and a pale steel-colored shade followed. A long pyramidal shadow slid down to the foot of Hermon and crept across the plain, seventy miles away, until at last it stood out as a dusky cone of darkness against the glowing sky, — the shadow of the mountain itself outlined against the illimitable heaven. The sun, dropping slowly through the western vapours, slid at length into the sea and vanished like a spark of fire. One by one the stars shone out overhead in Eastern brilliancy, and the night rested like a benediction upon the world.

The disciples were weary, weighed down with sleep. They folded their garments about them and rested, as an Oriental peasant can always do, upon the bare ground, under the roof of heaven. But Jesus prayed, — prayed for them, that their faith might receive some encouragement, that their eyes might be opened like the eyes of Elisha's servant, to see the invisible glories about them, — prayed for himself, that He might receive some fresh assurance of his Father's love and favour to strengthen and support his heart. And then, — as when a great light is kindled within a cathedral, and the dark windows are transformed into fountains of radiance blazing out into the night, — then, by some ebullition of spiritual splendour from within, the soul of Jesus sent out a flood of celestial light and He was transfigured. The celestial form shone through the earthly framework, so that his face was like the sun and his raiment glistering white as light. And with Him appeared Moses, whom God's own hand had laid in his secret grave on Nebo's lonely side, and Elijah, who had been carried in the chariot of fire into the heavenly world. These two greatest of the Old Testament saints, the representatives of the Law and the Prophets, appeared with Jesus, and " spake of his decease which He should accomplish at Jerusalem,"

Surely we cannot fail to see the purpose of this marvellous event. It was to uplift and cheer the soul of Jesus with the thought of the glory into which He should return by the sorrowful way of the cross. It was a foretaste of the exceeding great reward of his sacrificial love. It was a touch of the joy of heaven to help Him to bear the sufferings of earth. And it was an assurance of the sympathy of the celestial world with his great purpose of sacrifice and death. His disciples did not yet understand this purpose. They could not talk with Him about it in any such way as to help Him. They could only protest against it, and strive to restrain Him. But the saints in glory understood what He was doing. They bent from heaven to follow with loving, wondering eyes his steadfast journeyings towards the cross; and when they were permitted to speak with Him, they talked of that great, world-redeeming death from which his flesh shrank, but for which his divine heart was ready and longing.

There is a strange suggestiveness in this conversation. Who can tell how much the blessed dead know of our lives here upon earth! It may be that they are following our paths even now with wise and tender eyes, rejoicing in our victories, sympathizing with us in every noble endeavor, in every pure resolve, in every unselfish suffering for love.

> "There is no place where earth's sorrows
> Are more felt than up in heaven."

It may be that some saint dearer to you than any whose names are written among the Old Testament worthies — your own faithful mother, the father who prayed with you at the family altar, the friend who walked close beside you in the journey of life — is looking down upon you and watching your path to-day. And of this be sure: If you are following in the footsteps of Christ, if you are trying to do good, if you are sacrificing yourself for others, if you are treading the path of duty and devotion, these are the things which they understand, and for which they bless and love you. You may be misunderstood, you may be misrepresented by your friends on earth: but with everything that is good, with all noble suffering, there is perfect sympathy in heaven.

The disciples, who had been asleep when the Transfiguration began, were awake before it ended. The radiance shining about them opened their eyes; they roused themselves; they saw their Master in his glory; they heard the great lawgiver and the great prophet talking with Him about that death which seemed so incredible. It must have been an overwhelming, wonderful, joyous vision. It was in one sense a rebuke to their own weakness and want of sympathy, and yet this rebuke must have been almost swallowed up and forgotten in the glad assurance that their Master was indeed the Messiah. They must have looked with unspeakable awe, they must have listened with inexpressible delight. But when the vision began to fade, when the forms of the heavenly visitants grew dim before their departure, Peter could keep silence no longer; he felt that he must speak, though he knew not what to say. He cried, "Master, it is good for us to be here: and let us make three tabernacles; one for thee, and one for Moses, and one for Elias."

Now you will observe that this saying of Peter's may be divided into two parts. The first part is all right. It is perfectly true. It was good for them to be there. Otherwise, Christ would not have brought them there. It was a glorious and joyful and profitable hour. The memory of it was to remain with them all through their lives as a source of comfort and encouragement and strength. It was a good thing for Peter and James and John that they had been with their Master and seen his glory in the holy mount. But Peter made his mistake when he said, "Let us make three tabernacles and stay here forever."

I. It was a mistake, in the first place, to suppose that the building of the tabernacles would have done any good.

It would not have detained the fleeting vision, or perpetuated the transitory delight. Moses and Elias had to return to their places in the heavenly world. Jesus had to go down to the valley to heal the poor demoniac, and tread his appointed path to the cross. Peter and James and John had to take care of their families, and be prepared for their work as missionaries and martyrs of the gospel. The ecstasy could not be prolonged. The mountain-top must be deserted.

I have seen in the little English city of Salisbury the great cathedral. It was built when a flood-tide of religious enthusiasm was sweeping over the world. Thousands might worship, thousands have worshipped, within that splendid fane, and its walls were not able to contain the great flood of devotion. But the tide has ebbed; the ecstatic vision has faded. The mighty cathedral stands; but a handful of worshippers can scarcely keep a sleepy rivulet of praise flowing in a corner of the building. No tabernacle can detain a moment of religious enthusiasm; and if Peter and his friends had built the grandest cathedral in the world on the ridge of Mount Hermon, it might have been empty and bare to-day.

II. It was a mistake, in the second place, to suppose that the disciples had any right to remain on the glory-smitten summit and to enjoy the wondrous vision at their own pleasure.

It was a foretaste of heaven, but heaven belongs to God, and to those whom He has called to be with Him. Peter wanted to stay there before his time had come. He wanted to enjoy the rest, the blessedness, the glory of the celestial world before he had lived out his life and finished his work on earth. He wanted to have the crown without the cross.

How natural this is! How often we have felt like Peter! How often we have longed to escape from the turmoil and temptation of this evil world and dwell in some calm and lofty region of religious ecstasy, holding unbroken communion with God! This is the feeling that has often withdrawn the purest men and women from their duties in the working world to spend their lives in sweet contemplation amid the quietude of convents and monasteries. I suppose Bunyan's Pilgrim would gladly have stayed in the House Beautiful. I suppose he hated to go down from the Delectable Mountains. But he had to go. The only way to the heavenly city led through the rough valley and over the weary plain.

There is no gate into heaven except at the end of the path of duty. There is not even an honoured and peaceful grave for us until we can say with the Master, " I have glorified thee on the earth, I have finished the work thou gavest me to do."

III. It was a mistake, in the third place, to suppose that, because it was good for them to be there at one time, it would have been good for them to be there always.

Even if the vision could have tarried, even if God had permitted the tabernacles to be built, it would not have been best for Peter to abide on that mountain-top. It might have made him selfish and cold; it might have absorbed in the exercises of personal devotion all the warmth of that great, generous heart which God designed to use in making the world purer and better and happier. There was a deeper, richer blessing provided for Peter in the fellowship of suffering with Christ, and in the reward of faithful labour for the spread of the Master's kingdom of righteousness and peace and joy. So it came to pass that there was no answer to his foolish proposal; only a great silence, while the luminous cloud swept lower to enclose the three shining forms; and then a voice from the cloud, "This is my beloved Son, hear Him." Suddenly the vision had vanished; "they saw no man any more, save Jesus only with themselves;" and He led them down to help a poor, sick, human child in the valley, and deliver him from the evil spirits that tormented him.

My friends, there are two kinds of religion in the world, — the religion that is heavy with self, and the religion that is strong with love. There are some people who mix opium with their Christianity. It soothes and charms them; it gives them pleasant dreams and emotions; it lifts them above the world in joyous reveries. They would fain prolong them and dwell in them, and enjoy an unearned felicity. Their favourite hymn is, —

> "My willing soul would stay
> In such a frame as this,
> And sit and sing herself away
> To everlasting bliss."

But no one ever got to everlasting bliss by that method. The world has small need of a religion which consists solely or chiefly of emotions and raptures. But the religion that follows Jesus Christ, alike when He goes up into the high mountain to pray and when He comes down into the dark valley to work; the religion that listens to Him, alike when He tells us of the peace and joy of the Father's house and when He calls us to feed his lambs; the religion that is willing to suffer as well as to enjoy, to labour as well as to triumph; the religion that has a soul to worship God, and a heart to love man, and a hand to help in every good cause, — is pure and undefiled.

Try your religious emotions, your experiences of secret inward joy and peace, by this test. If they make you selfish, if you seek to prolong them unduly or excite them by artificial means, they are false and worthless. But if they make you kind and brave and helpful, if you are willing to come down from them, when you are called, to do hard, and distasteful, and even menial, work for your Master and your fellow-men, if the vision of faith has its fruits in the life of charity, then be thankful to Him who has revealed himself to you more clearly in order that you may love Him more dearly, and follow Him more faithfully in the service of humanity.

Remember that in this world every mountain-top of privilege is girdled by the vales of lowly duty.

Remember that the transfiguration of the soul is but the preparation and encouragement for the sacrifice of the life.

Remember that we are not to tarry in the transitory radiance of Mount Hermon, but to press on to the enduring glory of Mount Zion, and that we can only arrive at that final and blessed resting-place by the way of Mount Calvary.

Remember that Peter's mistake is corrected and explained by Peter's own words in the full experience of the school of Christ. For the Spirit of Jesus was in him, and taught him what to say, when he wrote at the close of his life: —

"Beloved, think it not strange concerning the fiery trial which is to try you, as though some strange thing happened unto you. But rejoice, inasmuch as ye are partakers of Christ's sufferings, that when his glory shall be revealed ye may be glad also with exceeding joy."

IX

GOD OVER ALL

"That ye may be the children of your Father which is in heaven; for He maketh his sun to rise on the evil and on the good, and sendeth rain on the just and on the unjust."

Matthew v. 45.

"He maketh his sun to rise on the evil and on the good, and sendeth rain on the just and on the unjust."

This is a simple statement of a familiar fact. We do not need any convention of scientists to assure us of its truth, nor any bulletin of the Weather Bureau to bear witness to its accuracy. A little experience is enough to convince us that what we call the processes of Nature are thoroughly impartial. They do not discriminate. They are quite regardless of moral character.

All through the summer that is past, the sun has been shining and the rain has been falling on the fields without regard to the moral or religious differences of their owners. There is no peculiar blessing on Protestant potatoes. The corn and pumpkins in the stingy farmer's fields are ripening just as surely and just as abundantly as those which have been planted and hoed by the most generous of men. All you have to do is to sow the seed and till the soil, and Nature will do the rest without asking what manner of man you are.

But is there not something strange about this fact? Familiar as it is, growing more and more plain to us, working itself more and more firmly into our experience the longer we live, when we stop to look at it and interrogate it more closely does it not puzzle and confound us? Does it not introduce a strange and, so to speak, irreligious element into our conception of the world and human life?

If we regarded Nature as impersonal, and the universe as a material mechanism, we should find no difficulty in it. For then this shining of the sun and falling of the rain upon the evil and the good, this procession of the seasons, this interflow of forces and influences which work together in productiveness, this germinating of the seed and unfolding of the blade and forming of the ear and ripening of the full corn in the ear, — the same for every child of man who toils and waits, — all this would be to us only the proof and illustration of what we should call the large indifference of Nature. What does she care for us or for our doings? She, the vast, impersonal, unimpassioned Being who is first our unfeeling mother, and then, when we have conquered her, our obedient slave, — we who are first her offspring, and then, when we are clever enough, her masters, — what does Nature care for us, or for those dreams of ours which we call virtue and vice? It all goes on by order and unconscious law. Suns rise and set. Clouds gather and sweep by. Tides ebb and flow. The dews descend and the grass springs. The grain-field changes from green to gold. The mellow apples ripen and fall. The vine feeds the deep purple of its clusters with the autumn's blood, and the many-foliaged forest clothes itself with a splendour of death. Man comes into the great world. He is weak but clever. He looks on Nature with his intelligent eyes, sees his advantage and follows it up. He makes the sun feed him and the animals work for him. He wanders through the world grasping its fruits as he can reach them, gathering with painful toil the slow results of a niggard year, or crushing with eager hands the rich grapes of plenty; and then, with the cry of want or song of gladness on his lips, he is gone; his place is empty, his grave is full, and suns shine and rains fall upon his tombstone even as they once shone and fell upon him. It is a wondrous pageant, but there is no meaning in it, no purpose in the play, no moral in the story, and we need not try to understand or explain it, because there is nothing to explain or understand, so long as Nature is unconscious and impersonal.

But the moment we see God behind the face of Nature,— the moment we believe that this vast and marvellous procession of seasons and causes and changes, this array of interworking forces, is directed and controlled by a Supreme, Omniscient, Holy Spirit, whose will is manifest in the springing of the seed, the ripening of the fruit, the fading of the leaf, the shining of the sun, and the falling of the rain,— this indifference becomes incomprehensible and impossible. It cannot be that God is indifferent. It cannot be that He cares not whether the dwellers upon his earth are wicked or righteous, foul or pure, selfish or generous. It cannot be that He looks down with the same feelings upon all who move below Him, and has an equal approbation for the toil of the honest labourer and the crafty schemes of the thief.

You tell me that Nature is indifferent. I say, Not if God is behind Nature.

You tell me that it matters not whether the hand that guides the plow be pure and clean, or wicked and defiled. Nature feels alike and will do alike for both. I say, Not if God is behind Nature, not if Nature is the expression of his will. He may do alike, but He does not feel alike. As well say that He who made light and darkness cannot distinguish between them, as that He whose will is the moral law ever forgets it, ignores it, casts it aside, in any sphere or mode of his action. Evermore He loves the good, the true, the noble. Evermore He hates the base, the false, the evil. Evermore iniquity is an abomination unto Him, and righteousness is his delight.

Why, then, does He not always discriminate in all his dealings? Why does the earth yield her increase as generously to the murderer as to the saint? Why do the glories of summer spread themselves as freely before the eyes of haggard wickedness as before the childlike eyes of innocence and love? Why is not the pathway of virtue always crowned with fragrance and light, and the way of vice dark and dreary with tempests and thorns? Why, since God is wise and just and sovereign, why does his sun shine and his rain fall equally upon the evil and good?

There is a meaning, there is a purpose in it, as in all his dealings. And what we need is the clear eye, the attentive mind, the enlightened heart, to discern and understand and accept it.

I. And, first of all, I think it is evident that He would thus teach us to believe in his Fatherhood in its widest aspect of benignity. He would manifest his abounding kindness to all the children of men. In the return of winter and summer, seed-time and harvest, in the constant delight and glory of Nature's pageant, and the bounteous results of the recurring seasons, He is opening his hand and supplying the wants of all his creatures. The open hand, not the blind eye nor the unfeeling heart, but the open hand, is the true symbol of God's dealing with mankind in the natural world. And this changes all, instantly and totally. Instead of the large indifference of Nature, we have the great beneficence of God. Instead of an unconscious mechanism, grinding out the same results and careless of the hands into which they fall, we have the wise and generous Father making ample and equal provision for all his children, bad and good. Do we not understand this? Do we not see the analogy and parallel in our human life?

In every family there may be children, perhaps not more and less beloved, but surely more and less approved. There are some that come closer to the father's heart, obedient, generous, affectionate; answering every call upon their love; rendering swift, unconscious services of help and comfort; weaving themselves into the very inmost life, and growing dearer with every day and year. And there are some that cannot or will not come so near; cold, dull, irresponsive; set chiefly upon the following of their own wills and the pleasing of their own desires; living by their own choice and disposition farther and farther away from those that gave them birth, and sometimes wilfully wounding and bruising the hearts to which they ought to be most closely bound. Is it possible that the father should feel alike towards both? He cannot and does not. Even though he does not speak of it, even though he does not show it, there is a vast, a world-wide difference.

And yet they are all his children. For all of them his heart is tender and his care watchful. And for all of them he will provide with an impartial benevolence. It is a point of honour with him. He will do the best he can for all. He will defend their helplessness, and provide for their needs, and keep the sweet shelter of home around them all, for are they not all his children?

Are we not also the offspring of God? Yes, every one of us, the lowest as well as the highest. He is the Father of us all.

We do not dare to think that there is even one forgotten, despised, disowned. God will not let us think so. With clear, sweet, but silent voice, He is assuring every child of man that the heavens above his head are not empty, but filled with the presence of a Divine Father, and that the earth beneath his feet is not a strange and desert place, but the soil of his own home, in which paternal bounty will make provision for his wants. Every ray of sunlight that falls from heaven, every drop of rain that waters the fruitful ground, is saying to the heart of man, "My child, this a Father's impartial kindness sends to thee."

If men would only hear it! Oh that the deaf ear and the dull heart might be touched and opened to the beautiful speech of the seasons, so that plenty might draw all souls to gratitude, and beauty move all spirits to worship, and every fair landscape, and every overflowing harvest, and every touch of loveliness and grace upon the face of the world, might lift all souls that live and feel from Nature up to Nature's God! This is what He longs for. This is what He means when He tells us, in his impartial sunshine and rain, that He is the Father of all mankind.

II. But I think it is clear also that God uses this large impartiality in the gifts of Nature to teach us that this world is not a place of judgment, but a place of probation, in which the good and the evil are working side by side, not only in the same community but in the same character, and not to be finally separated until they have produced their fixed and final results. Discriminations and judgments in regard to qualities and actions are to a certain extent necessary. We say of self-sacrifice that it is good. We say of lying that it is evil. We call some men pure and noble. We call others base and wicked. But we do not say of any living, breathing human being, "That is a lost, hopeless sinner, with nothing but evil in him."

We dare not say it, for God himself does not say it. The parable of the wheat and the tares applies not only to the world at large, but also, and just as truly, to the individual soul. It is only in novels that the villains are absolutely bad, while the heroes and heroines are immaculately good. In real life, men and women are all somewhat mixed, and every soul is more or less an enigma to itself.

We look into our own hearts and we are puzzled. We cannot interpret all that is within them. The strange mingling flow of impulses and emotions and desires, the undercurrent of half-unconscious motives and the after-play of repentance and regret, making the colour of our actions change with the changing light,—all this troubles and confuses us. We cry in all sincerity, "I cannot understand myself. There is something here that I cannot judge." And from the shining sun and the falling rain comes the clear, kind, patient voice of God, "Neither do I judge thee yet. Not yet is thy final place assigned. Not yet is thy trial ended. The days of life are still thine. The sun still shines and the rain still falls upon thy fields. Thou mayest be sunken deep in evil, but thou still hast hope, for behold I spare thee still, I still am waiting. I do not judge thee yet."

"Not yet," "not yet,"—how solemnly the warning of these words mingles with the sweet assurance of a lingering hope for every child of man! How clearly the patient refusal to judge now, reveals the certainty that God will judge hereafter! If this world is only a place of probation, then beyond it there must be a place of judgment. If, in the distribution of this world's goods, the wicked and the righteous fare alike; if it sometimes seems that the wicked fare even better in their iniquity, while in the proudness of their heart they wax fat,—then surely, in the world to come, the just God must make compensation. Dishonesty, and cruelty, and selfish lust will receive their punishment at the end. The sweet sun will not shine forever, and the cool rain will not always fall upon the evil-doers. Nor shall those who have waited patiently and lived purely fail of their reward. God cannot disinherit them. Their harvest will surely come in the world of light.

How precious, then, how costly and invaluable, is every day and hour of this mortal life in which the warm sunlight and the gentle rain assure us that the upward way is still open to us! We may still sow that good seed which shall bear fruit unto eternal life. But how long, for you and me, how long shall this time of hope endure? The night cometh. Who can tell?

III. Once more, I think that God deals thus kindly with the evil as well as with the good, in order to make known to all men the length and breadth of his forgiving love. The length and breadth, not the height and depth of it, for that could only be expressed in Jesus Christ, coming down from heaven to die for the world. Thus only could the fulness of God's love be manifest.

But something of its largeness, some shadowing forth of its generosity and freedom, can be discovered in the process of Nature.

> "There's a wideness in God's mercy
> Like the wideness of the sea."

Yes, and like the spreading glories of the sunset, and like the flowing of a great river, and like the dropping of the gentle dew from heaven. These all tell us, and tell us truly, of the heart of God, who is willing to forgive, and longing to do good unto all men. It is narrated of the great novelist, Thackeray, that he was once walking with a friend at evening on the hills near Edinburgh. The sun sank slowly to his rest, leaving a trail of glory behind him, and the solemn splendours of the sky deepened above the crowded tenements, the dark, foul, noisome streets, the pain and misery and want, of the old town. Thackeray looked at it long in silence, and then, turning to his companion with tears in his eyes, he said, "Calvary."

Think of it, friends! God bestows all the beauty and all the loveliness of the world upon sinners such as we are. Even though we have disobeyed Him and rebelled against Him, his hand still feeds us. Even though our hearts are filled with vileness, his pure-eyed stars look down on us in tenderness and compassion. Even though we should wander far away and forget Him, and steep ourselves in wickedness, his sun would still shine, his rain would still fall for us. Look up, look up, thou prodigal child, lost to thyself and to thy home, sunken in vice and full of inward misery, thou art not lost to thy Father. For lo! with every morning above thine evil and unhappy head,

"God makes himself an awful rose of dawn."

And even as his light follows and caresses thee wherever thou mayest roam, so his love is close to thee, and his mercy waiting to welcome thee, if thou wilt but turn to Him.

But are there not also some practical lessons which we, as Christians, may learn from God's impartial and generous distribution of the gifts of nature? Is there not a sweet and gentle instruction for the daily life to be derived from the sun which shines and the rain which falls alike upon the evil and upon the good? Our Divine Master thought there was, and used this lovely parable to convey a most precious lesson to the hearts of his disciples, a lesson of charity and patience and forgiving love.

For surely this proof of the Fatherhood of God ought to deepen in our hearts the sense of the Brotherhood of man. When we see Him providing with equal hands for all men, causing the grass to spring and the flowers to bloom and the stars to shine for the whole world, treating even the outcast and despised of men with impartial kindness, surely we ought to feel more profoundly and more tenderly the ties which bind together all those whom God hath made of one blood to dwell together on the face of the earth. Our artificial life, the life which seems inseparable from the advance of civilization and the growth of large cities, tends to deepen and exaggerate what we call "class distinctions." It keeps men far apart from each other, creates misunderstanding and distrust. Too often it awakens evil passions of pride and contempt among the rich, to be met by the equally evil passions of envy and hatred among the poor. When we feel these influences stealing over us, when we find that we are learning to think of ourselves and our friends as the finest porcelain and of the rest of mankind as common clay, when we begin to reckon the worth of manhood and womanhood by the possession of wealth and the richness of attire, then it is well for us to

> "Go forth into the light of things;
> Let Nature be our teacher."

See how God's great sun laughs at our pride, shining with equal radiance upon the cottage and upon the palace, and painting for the eyes of all richer pictures than the wealth of Crœsus can buy. See how God's sweet rain ignores our vanity, falling as gently and as generously upon the poor child's box of mignonette in the window as upon the costliest roses in the parterre. See how all things that God has made tell us of an impartial Father's love which ought to waken in our hearts a brother's kindness for our fellow-men.

But more than this, we ought to learn from the truth so simply expressed in the text and so often illustrated before our eyes. We ought to see in God's forbearance to judge men a lesson of forbearance to us.

We are too quick: not often too quick to

approve, but very often too quick to condemn. We think it confers a sort of dignity and virtue to say of other men and women that they are bad. We are in haste to don the judicial ermine and put on the black cap and pronounce sentence. We foster evil reports, and repeat gossip, and devour our fellows like cannibals. Who art thou that judgest another? Remember Christ's words to the scribes and Pharisees. Remember his words to his own disciples, "Judge not, that ye be not judged." How can we read the hidden motives, how can we know the deep repentance and regret that enter into the lives about us? Beware of censoriousness. This world of impartial sunlight and equal falling rain is not the place of judgment. And, thank God, you and I are not, either here or hereafter, the final judges. My heart would shrink in speechless terror from deciding the destiny of a single human soul. That belongs to God; and to God not now, but when the shadows of time have been lost in the light of eternity.

Finally, my friends, when we see God forgiving all men who have sinned against Him, sparing them in his mercy, and showering his bounty alike upon the evil and the good, let us take the gracious lesson of forgiveness to our hearts. Why should we hate like Satan when we may forgive like God? Why should we cherish malice, envy, and all uncharitableness in our breasts? I know that some people use us despitefully and show themselves our enemies, but why should we fill our hearts with their bitterness and inflame our wounds with their poison? This world is too sweet and fair to darken it with the clouds of anger. This life is too short and precious to waste it in bearing that heaviest of all burdens, a grudge. Forgive and forget if you can; but *forgive* anyway; and pray heartily and kindly for all men, for thus only shall we be the children of our Father who maketh his sun to rise on the evil and on the good, and sendeth rain on the just and on the unjust.

X

THE HORIZON

"The secret things belong unto the Lord our God: but those things which are revealed belong unto us and to our children forever, that we may do all the words of this law."

Deuteronomy xxix. 29.

"The secret things belong unto the Lord our God: but those things which are revealed belong unto us and to our children forever, that we may do all the words of this law."

THERE is no landscape which is not bounded by the horizon. This fact is the symbol of a profound truth. It reminds us that our powers are finite and limited. However high we may climb to win a wider outlook, our vision will touch its confines and the known will be ringed about by the unknown. This is the Doctrine of the Horizon.

Now the text applies this truth to religion. It speaks of things revealed and declares that they belong to us. And in speaking thus it appeals to our religious instinct, our spiritual common-sense. For a religion which contained no real disclosure of the divine to our minds and hearts would have no meaning and therefore no value. The horizon must include something. It is idle to talk of the religious sentiments of awe, reverence, humility, and gratitude as if they could exist without any known motive or object. That of which we are, and must remain, altogether ignorant can never influence our belief, our worship, or our conduct.

A religion all mystery is a light all darkness. It does not help us in the least when a philosopher spells the Unknowable with a capital U and advises us to worship It. For when we ask him what to believe about It, he can only answer, "Believe that you can never know what It is;" and when we ask him what to say to It, he can only answer "Say nothing;" and when we ask him what It would have us do for Its glory, he can only answer, "You must find out for yourself, for It will never tell you." A religion of this kind, a religion of the Unknowable, is a large name for something which has no existence: it is an idle word dancing recklessly on the brink of nonsense. Certainly it is not the religion of the Bible which discloses a God who has made himself known unto men; nor of Paul, who said, "Whom therefore ye ignorantly worship, Him declare we unto you;" nor of Christ, who said to the Samaritans, "Ye worship ye know not what: we know what we worship."

But the text also speaks of secret things, and affirms that they belong unto the Lord our God. This also is a reasonable voice and one that carries conviction to our spirit. For certainly a religion that professed to reveal and explain everything, and to make the moral order of the universe and the nature and plans of God as plain to our comprehension as a map of the United States, — a religion that contained no mystery, would be quite as incredible as a religion that was all mystery. We find insoluble problems and undiscoverable secrets in nature, and we expect to find them in theology. There is something hidden even in the least and lowest form of life, why not also in the highest and greatest? Do you remember Tennyson's poem of "The Flower"?

> "Flower in the crannied wall,
> I pluck you out of the crannies,
> I hold you here, root and all, in my hand,
> Little flower — but *if* I could understand
> What you are, root and all, and all in all,
> I should know what God and man is."

But that is precisely what we cannot attain: a perfect comprehension, a complete knowledge, a vision without a horizon, even in regard to the smallest things. And if we do not look for this in the realm of the finite, surely we cannot dream of reaching it in the realm of the Infinite. Anything that a telescope could discover among the stars, anything that logic could define and explain and fit into an exact philosophical system, would not be God. For it belongs to his very essence that He transcends our thought, and that his judgments are unsearchable and his ways past finding out. We do not know anything about God unless we know that we cannot know Him perfectly.

Modest ignorance is a necessary element of true theology. Bishop Butler says, "The monarchy of the Universe is a dominion unlimited in extent and everlasting in duration: the general system of it must therefore be quite beyond our comprehension." Richard Hooker says, "We know not God as He is, neither can know Him. His glory is inexplicable, his greatness above our capacity and reach." And this is but an echo of the majestic language of the Bible: "It is as high as heaven; what canst thou do? deeper than hell; what canst thou know? The measure thereof is longer than the earth and broader than the sea." "For we know in part and we prophesy in part. But when that which is perfect is come, then that which is in part shall be done away."

The partial knowledge of divine things, the line which divides God's secrets from his revelations, the necessary horizon of religious thought, — this is the subject to which I would call your attention. Let us observe the fact that it exists, and the dangers of trying to go beyond it, and the advantages of keeping within it.

I. It is a simple fact that we cannot know all about God. Natural theology, of course, is limited. Revealed theology widens the boundaries of our knowledge, but does not abolish them. The Bible does not profess to make men omniscient, but simply to tell them enough to make them happy and good, if they will believe it and live up to it. It does indeed lift man above the level of his natural ignorance; but even as one who has gained a wider view of the world by ascending a lofty mountain still finds his sight circumscribed by a new horizon, so those who receive the revelations which are contained in Holy Scripture still discover a verge beyond which their thought cannot pass, and find themselves shut in by the secret things which belong unto God. Indeed, this fact of limitation is itself one of the things revealed. Not to the sea alone, but also to the questioning intellect of man does God say, "Hitherto shalt thou come, but no further: and here shall thy proud waves be stayed."

Take your Bible, and see how far it leads you on, and how firmly it holds you back; how much it discloses, and how much it hides. Everywhere you can see the horizon line running sharply around the things revealed and hiding the things secret.

In regard to God himself, it seems to me that his character is revealed and his essence is secret. His moral attributes are made known to us so that we cannot mistake them. He is just and holy, merciful and compassionate, bountiful and loving, and He discloses these qualities so fully in his self-revelation in Jesus Christ that they become clear and distinct and indubitable to us; they belong to us and to our children forever. We know Him as the Father of our spirits, for Jesus Christ says, "He that hath seen me hath seen the Father." But his metaphysical attributes, the ground and mode and form of his existence, are behind the veil. Omniscience, Omnipresence, Omnipotence, — when we speak these words we do not define God, we simply name the limits of our thought about Him. They are lines which run out into infinity; and when we try to follow them with our logic, they lead us into a region where argument is vain and definition is absurd. Do you remember what Moses saw in the mount? He said unto the Lord, "I beseech thee show me thy glory." But God answered, "I will make all my goodness pass before thee." Here is the boundary-line of knowledge: God's goodness is revealed; but his glory is beyond the horizon.

And does not the same line run between the purposes of God which He has declared in Jesus Christ and the means of executing those purposes? We believe that God is the Ruler of the universe, and that He intends that his will shall be done on earth even as it is done in heaven. It is his will to punish the wicked and to reward the righteous; to judge the obstinate and to have mercy upon the penitent; to vanquish the evil and to establish the good; to destroy death and him that hath the power of death, that is, the devil, and in the fulness of time to gather together in one all things in Christ, both which are in heaven and which are on earth. Nothing could be more certain to those who believe in God than this mighty purpose. But nothing could be more inscrutable than the manner of its accomplishment. We know that God is sovereign. We know also that man is free, for the whole gospel is an appeal to his power of choice; the offer of pardon and life would be an absurdity, a deception, a moral mockery if he were not able to receive or to reject it at will. Both truths are revealed, both are sure and precious. But they come together in a line which is the absolute boundary of our vision, even as the ocean and the sky meet, but do not mingle, at the edge of the world. That is the horizon. Beyond that we cannot see.

What is all this reasoning and syllogizing about an eternal decree which determines the fate of every soul, this logical analysis of the relations between the human spirit which must be passive and the Divine Spirit which is given unto them who are appointed unto life and not unto them who are appointed unto death, — what is it all but a vain effort to go beyond the horizon?

Here is the sea on which you float, the sea of human life, with its shifting tides and currents. Yonder is the sky that bends above you, the pure and sovereign will of God. Out of that unsearchable heaven comes the breath of the Spirit, like "the wind that bloweth where it listeth, and thou canst not tell whence it cometh and whither it goeth." If you will spread your sail to catch that breath of life, if you will lay your course and keep your rudder true, you will be carried onward in peace and safety to your desired haven. Nay, more: if there seems to be no breeze stirring near you, if you feel that you are lying idle and help-less in a dead calm, drifting upon the dark currents which may bear you to destruction, you have only to ask for the saving breath and it will come. For earthly parents are not more willing to give good gifts unto their children than your Heavenly Father to give his Spirit unto them that ask Him. Ask, then, ask for what you can surely have, and sail, and steer, and leave the secret things to God.

Again, we may see the line of division running between the laws of God which are revealed and the final judgment of God which is secret. He has shown us what He would have us do. "What doth the Lord require of thee, but to do justly, and to love mercy, and to walk humbly with thy God?" He has declared that He will reward every man according to his works. He has made known the riches of his grace, his willingness to forgive the penitent, and to help the fallen, in Jesus Christ; and by the same lips He has made known his indignation against those who will not repent, nor trust in his mercy, nor show to others that love which God has shown to them. Nothing could be more clear and positive than the revelation of duty which God makes to each one of us. We must forsake our sins and deny ourselves, and take up our cross and follow Christ if we would be saved.

But beyond that is the region of secrets.

When we try to peer into it and explore it with our little lamps of reason, when we ask how God will deal with the heathen, who have not had our privileges and opportunities, when we inquire what is to become of this man or that man in the eternal future, we are simply going beyond the horizon. The very attempt to pronounce final judgment on our fellow-creatures implies what Butler has well called "the infinitely absurd supposition that we know the whole of the case." One thing is certain, God will never do injustice to a single soul, "but in every nation he that feareth Him and worketh righteousness is accepted with Him." The rest we may leave in silence with God; for judgment is his province, and there we may not intrude.

> "Let not this weak unknowing hand
>   Presume thy bolts to throw,
> And deal damnation round the land
>   On each I judge thy foe.
>
> "If I am right, thy grace impart
>   Still in the right to stay:
> If I am wrong, oh, teach my heart
>   To find that better way."

II. Let us think now of some of the evils

and dangers of going beyond the horizon in theology.

First of all, it is a dangerous thing because it is likely to lead to mistakes and errors. When a man sets out to be wise above what is written, he is in a fair way to arrive at folly; and when he endeavours to deal with infinite quantities by a finite logic his conclusions are apt to be absurd. It is better to know nothing about a subject, than to know something about it which is not so. It is wiser to stand in silent awe before the secret things which belong to God, than it is to adventure rashly among them and discover truths which do not exist.

The evil genius of religious thought is insatiable curiosity, and her handmaid is necessary deduction, and her kingdom is a kingdom of logical consistency and moral confusion. The plague of Christendom has been the passion of theology to define what God has not defined, and to discover what He has kept secret.

Take a few examples of this kind of work. The sacrifice of Christ is revealed to us in Scripture as a redemption of sinners. The curious theologizer, fixing upon this word redemption, follows it out beyond the horizon. A redemption is a price paid for something. If God has paid a price for the soul of man, it must have belonged to somebody else. The only other conceivable owner is Satan. Therefore, the death of Christ was a ransom paid to the devil for the soul of man. This amazing discovery of logic among the secret things was taught in the church for centuries.

Again, omniscience is declared to be one of the divine attributes. It means simply that God's wisdom is perfect, and therefore beyond our comprehension. But the inquisitive explorer takes this word as a raft and pushes out into the unknown. Omniscience, according to his definition, means that God knows everything from all eternity. If He foreknows everything, everything must be foreordained. If everything is foreordained, then the sin and death of every wicked man must be predetermined. If these things are predetermined, then God must have willed that they should come to pass; and if He has willed it, He must have decreed it. Therefore, "by the decree of God, for the manifestation of his glory, some men and angels are foreordained unto everlasting death, and these men and angels are particularly and unchangeably designed, and their number is so certain and definite that it can neither be increased or diminished." Thus the explorer of Omniscience reports his discovery; and when we turn from his report to the Bible, which tells us of "God, who is not willing that any should perish, but that all should come to repentance," we feel that the explorer has gone a long way beyond the horizon and has discovered something which is probably not true.

Again, the Bible reveals the fact of the second coming of Christ, but it declares at the same time that the day and the hour of his advent are hidden from all men. Now here is a horizon distinctly and divinely established, and yet good people have not been able to restrain their curiosity from trying to pass over it. They have counted the numbers in the book of Daniel, and discovered that Napoleon Bonaparte was the man of sin. They have investigated the horns of the various allegorical creatures and the clothing of the scarlet woman in the book of the Revelation, and identified the Pope as the antichrist. They have fixed with more or less particularity the date of the millennium, and have assembled in white robes to wait for its arrival — but it failed to arrive, because it is still beyond the horizon.

Of all the activities in which men have employed their intellect, there is none which has produced such a large amount of incorrect information and erroneous discovery, as this habit of pushing beyond the horizon into the secrets of God.

Moreover, it is an undesirable habit because it leads to bitter strife and controversy. There is no opinion for which men are so ready to fight as one in regard to which there is room for considerable uncertainty. Almost all of the conflicts in Christian thought — and many of the most bloody schisms in the Christian Church — have been in the region of speculation rather than in the region of faith. In regard to the great essential truths which are clearly revealed there has been substantial unity from the beginning. But when men have begun to make their inferences and deductions from these truths, when they have tried to run them out beyond the horizon, and to map out the universe according to a fixed system, then divisions have appeared, and anathemas and counter-anathemas have filled the air, and the music of worship has been broken by the clash of swords. "What are these people quarrelling about?" asks the plain man. They are quarrelling, my beloved brother, for the most part about the things that none of them can understand. Being unwilling to let God have any secrets, they are unable to let men have any peace. This is one of the results of going beyond the horizon.

But even if this result does not follow, even if speculation upon the secret things is carried on peaceably and charitably, it is at best an idle habit and therefore undesirable. Vast quantities of time have been wasted in pursuing investigations into the nature and the plans of God which cannot possibly concern us, or have any appreciable influence upon our virtue or our happiness. I have heard lately of an ecclesiastical assembly which spent many hours in discussing what God ought to do with idiots in the future life. Not content with the question in its general aspect, they specified the case of a man who had been in the possession of his reason until the age of twenty-five, and then, by accident or disease, had been reduced to idiocy. This problem they debated as gravely and as exhaustingly as if it had been committed to them for decision. I do not know what conclusion they arrived at, nor do I think that it is of any particular consequence whether they arrived at any conclusion. The most desirable thing was that they should come to an end.

The trouble with most of our Confessions of Faith and Articles of Religion is that they are too long. They contain the system of doctrine taught in the Holy Scriptures; but they contain also a great deal more. And these additions, inferences, and deductions have always been the most costly to attain, the most perilous to defend, the most difficult to believe, and the least profitable to apply.

The first lesson to be learned by one who would think wisely or speak truly of religious questions is to say, in regard to the secret things, "I do not know, and I shall not try to guess." The advice which Milton puts into the speech of the affable archangel Raphael is prudent, and as good for us as it was for Adam.

> "Solicit not thy thoughts with matters hid;
> Leave them to God above, him serve and fear:
> Of other creatures, as him pleases best,
> Wherever placed, let him dispose: joy thou
> In what he gives to thee, this paradise,
> And thy fair Eve; Heaven is for thee too high
> To know what passes there. Be lowly wise;
> Think only what concerns thee and thy being;
> Contented that thus far hath been revealed,
> Not of earth only, but of highest Heaven."

III. Think now for a moment of the great benefits which will come to us from following this advice. Think of the large blessings of a small theology. Think of the advantages of being confined to, and contented with, the things that are revealed, without trying to go beyond the horizon.

It will deliver us from perplexing thoughts which interrupt the sweetness of life. It will leave us free to enjoy the good gifts of God. Above all, it will enable us to devote our best thought, our deepest energy, our strongest faith to the apprehension and application of those great, simple, vital truths which God has made known for the salvation of our souls and the uplifting of the world into the heavenly life. That is what we need, and that is what the text means, — apprehension and application of the great simple truths of religion within the horizon.

The things that are revealed belong unto us and to our children forever, — is not that what our hearts desire and crave? A religion which shall really belong to us, be a part of us, enter into us, abide with us, and not with us only, but with our children, forever. Not many doctrines, but solid. It need not be very wide, but it must be very deep. It must go down to the bottom of our hearts and dwell there as a living certainty. To be sure of God, most wise, most mighty, most holy, most loving, our Father in heaven and on earth; to be sure of Christ, divine and human, our Brother and our Master, the pattern of excellence and the Redeemer from sin, the Saviour of all who trust in Him; to be sure of the Holy Spirit, the Comforter, the Guide, the Purifier, given to all who ask for Him; to be sure of immortality, an endless life in which nothing can separate us from the love of God, — my friends, let us concentrate our faith upon these things. If we can get hold of these profound realities, if we can gather about them all the forces of reason and conscience and experience and testimony to establish them forever, if we can rest upon them firmly and steadfastly, feeling that they are ours because they are revealed, we shall be satisfied. For our great need is not to know more about religion, but to be more sure of what we know.

There is but one way to attain this. We must live up to what we know. Our text concludes by saying "that we may do all the words of this law." Goodness is the purpose of religion, and its best proof. Conduct is the end of faith, and its strongest support. God has revealed himself in Christ in order that we may love Him and live with Him and be like Him. If we will do this we shall be sure of Him, and help other men to be sure of Him too. The best evidences of religion are holy and kind and useful and godly lives, really moulded and controlled by the divine Christ. A short creed well believed and honestly applied is what we need. The world waits, and we must pray and labour, not for a more complete and logical Theology, but for a more real and true and living Christianity.

The best thing that we can do to help the world to believe in a Divine Revelation is simply this: Trust in Jesus Christ, love our fellow-men, and follow Him in the path of daily duty.

www.ingramcontent.com/pod-product-compliance
Lightning Source LLC
Chambersburg PA
CBHW020801230426
43666CB00007B/796